T0198667

Reviews for Gifts of Guidance

As I prepared myself to choose a message from Gifts of Guidance – Fifty Messages, I asked a question from my heart. The answer not only pleasantly surprised me but inspired me to re-frame my perspective on the issue in question. Gifts of Guidance is truly a blessing that I am grateful to have access to.

Constance Solomon
CEO A1R Psychic Radio Network www.ask1radio.com

I've been a Liz Winter fan for many years, and I am so delighted that her wonderful new book, *Gifts of Guidance*, is finding its way into the world. Liz has created a rich tapestry of support for us with her angel guidance, combined with evocative imagery. But more than that, she offers us herself – her practical insights into psychic ability, and how her journey with her spirit guide White Owl unfolded. Her down-to-earth approach to all matters psychic and spiritual is comforting.

There is a sense of ease around the advice Liz offers that comes only with many years of practising an art. As well as sharing part of her story, and with the Angels and Archangels' guidance, she also gives us her 'momentary meditations', tiny moments out of the hectic pace of life, in which to re-balance.

For anyone in need, read this book! It will reach out to you in a gentle way, providing for me, yet more proof that there is only a very thin veil between this world and the next. With *Gifts of Guidance*, and in the company of a practitioner as compassionate and understanding as Liz, we are in good hands.

Candida Baker
candidabaker.com
www.verandahmagazine.com.au

Liz Winter once again weaves her loving magic through fifty diverse messages of wisdom in such an innovative way that will make her new book a must-have in our busy lives.

This book contains not only messages from her Messengers but also life lessons, advice, brief meditations and insights into Liz's own life experiences.

Choose a number and read what you need to hear about a current situation, or simply as a message to inspire you for the day.

Robyn Sutcliffe
Editor

GIFTS OF GUIDANCE

Fifty Messages

LIZ WINTER

BALBOA.
PRESS
A DIVISION OF HAY HOUSE

Copyright © 2017 Liz Winter.

All rights reserved. No part of this book may be used or reproduced by any means, graphic, electronic, or mechanical, including photocopying, recording, taping or by any information storage retrieval system without the written permission of the author except in the case of brief quotations embodied in critical articles and reviews.

Balboa Press books may be ordered through booksellers or by contacting:

Balboa Press
A Division of Hay House
1663 Liberty Drive
Bloomington, IN 47403
www.balboapress.com.au
1 (877) 407-4847

Because of the dynamic nature of the Internet, any web addresses or links contained in this book may have changed since publication and may no longer be valid. The views expressed in this work are solely those of the author and do not necessarily reflect the views of the publisher, and the publisher hereby disclaims any responsibility for them.

The author of this book does not dispense medical advice or prescribe the use of any technique as a form of treatment for physical, emotional, or medical problems without the advice of a physician, either directly or indirectly. The intent of the author is only to offer information of a general nature to help you in your quest for emotional and spiritual well-being. In the event you use any of the information in this book for yourself, which is your constitutional right, the author and the publisher assume no responsibility for your actions.

Any people depicted in stock imagery provided by Thinkstock are models, and such images are being used for illustrative purposes only.
Certain stock imagery © Thinkstock.

Print information available on the last page.

ISBN: 978-1-5043-0888-5 (sc)
ISBN: 978-1-5043-0887-8 (e)

Balboa Press rev. date: 06/20/2017

CONTENTS

ACKNOWLEDGEMENTS

My sincere and loving thanks to the Messengers in Spirit who graced me with their presence while writing Gifts of Guidance. A special thanks to my Spirit Guide, White Owl, for having faith in me.

Special and heartfelt thanks go out to:

Robyn Sutcliffe - my angel of editing and helpful feedback.

Lesa Corrine - for allowing me to use her magical photography.

Meadow Linn - for sharing her generous spirit through the insights she shares in the Foreword.

And, to all who read this book, may your life unfold with love, beauty, and grace!

Photography by Lesa Corrine

Lesa Corrine is an Australian-based photographer whose images are not only visually stunning, but evoke a sense of wonder from all who witness her art. Cover image and images within these pages by Lesa Corrine. Cover image photographed at The Blue Mountains NSW.
See more of Lesa's work at
www.photographybycorrine.zenfolio.com

FOREWORD

While on vacation with my family in Spain a number of years ago, a man appeared in my dream. He said, 'Please tell your mother that Caroline went to the light.' My mom's friend had been sick, but I was only vaguely aware of her illness, so there is no way that my conscious or even subconscious could have made this up. In the remote village where we were staying, it was difficult to reach us through conventional methods. (This was before Wi-Fi and cell phones were ubiquitous.) So, clearly, the powers-that-be took it upon themselves to find another means of getting through to us.

That morning, before I even had a chance to share the message with my mom, she said, 'I think Caroline may have died last night.' She'd woken up with an inner-knowing that her friend was at peace. Eventually, when we were able to get to an Internet cafe, my mom received e-mail with the news we already knew.

Love and guidance are available to us … always. We just have to be open to receiving. Sometimes, like when my family was in Spain, the message wants to be heard so badly that it makes its way into your consciousness all on its own. However, other times, we have to ask for assistance. As the saying goes, 'Ask and you shall receive.' I experienced this quite poignantly a couple years ago.

I really, really wanted a relationship. I couldn't figure it out. I was doing everything seemingly right. But, nothing was working. So, one evening before bed I decided to ask Spirit for help. That night I dreamed I was in a relationship! However, the man was completely different from what I'd been seeking. When I woke up I realized that even though I thought I'd been doing everything 'right,' I'd been closing myself off to the possibility of love coming in a different package. Within weeks, I'd found a man very similar to the one in my dream but very different from what I'd previously envisioned for myself. It didn't end up being my forever relationship, but we had a really good run. And it was all because of the message I received in my dream.

There have been other times in my life, however, when I've asked for a message or guidance, and it feels as though there's nothing but radio silence. This doesn't necessarily mean that messages aren't being transmitted. It just means I'm not hearing them or I'm tuned to a different frequency, like on the radio. Luckily, there's no need to fret when we can't hear the whispers from beyond. Liz Winter has done the work for us. She's created this beautiful book filled with amazing wisdom and powerful insights. The answers are right here, between your fingertips.

Liz offers a number of suggestions on how to use this book, ranging from opening randomly to a page for a general message to asking a specific question. Alternatively, you can choose a number that feels right and look up the associated message. That's what I did ... Wow! The message was spot-on.

The deadline for my next cookbook has been looming over me like a constant shadow. Suddenly it hit me! I can use *Gifts of Guidance* to alleviate some of my angst and gain clarity on how it will all unfold. As I closed my eyes and held the book between my hands, I thought about my cookbook. The number 37 came floating into my mind. So, I flipped through the pages until I came to Message #37. It couldn't have been more perfect!

Here is what it said:

'The period of metaphorically holding your breath or waiting in anticipation for an outcome is now ending. The winds of change now appear to create new scenarios that offer abundant consequences. Your consistent patience and faith reward you now and you can begin to count your blessings. [...] You have a positive message to share with others, possibly in the public arena. The power of expression accompanies the Bluebird spirit and is here to support you at this time. [...] Be assured that all is working out for the best and in divine timing.'

A whoosh of calm washed over me. Everything is unfolding just as intended...and in divine timing. *Gifts of Guidance* is more than a book of channelled wisdom; it's an oracle that provides reassurance, love, and support. It's no longer necessary to wait for messages to appear in your sleep or signs to appear while you go about your day. With this book, you have the opportunity to gain insights at any given moment, simply by opening the pages.

I will continue to open my heart to receiving messages like the one that came to me in Spain, and I will keep asking Spirit to provide support through my dreams, but now I also have this fabulous book for the times when I need a message right away and for when I just can't seem to tune in to the other side. I'm grateful to Liz for creating such a fun, easy-to-use, and meaningful book. *Gifts of Guidance* will be on my shelves for years to come.

Meadow Linn
Author of 'Soups to Savor'
Co Author of 'The Mystic Cookbook'
www.MeadowLinn.com

INTRODUCTION

Wisdom, swirling in a spiral cloud of white light, began to form into the shape of a male face. The energy was calm and brought a sense of familiarity. It felt like home. As pink, yellow, and blue swans glided across shimmering still water, reflecting the colours of a rainbow, I knew I had arrived in a special place. It was *my* special place, a place within me that I had created many years ago through the power of visualisation.

There are no limits in one's special place – created by the mind, visualised, sensed and breathed into being – it is a place anyone can create and visit. Yet it is more than that, it is where one can heal, communicate with the Spirit world and where one can clarify and manifest intentions. There are no limits, only the limitations of our imaginations. Once created, our inner sanctuary can be renovated or redesigned. By returning to your special place again and again, energy is built up that is exclusively in alignment with your vibration. It is a place that can bridge the Earth and Spirit world; it can connect your mind and soul, allow creativity to flow, solutions to emerge and comfort to be felt.

As I arrived in my special place, a wise face revealed itself to be my beautiful Spirit guide, White Owl. He greeted me with a wave of genuine love and gestured for me to sit by a stream on the soft, lime green grass. Two large Maple trees magically appeared behind our backs for support and nourishment.

White Owl's inquisitive brown eyes looked deeply into mine and a conversation began without words. He impressed upon me his compassion and understanding that my busy life had temporarily taken me away from my love of writing. 'I want to write another book White Owl, but I have so many ideas coming in at once and I can't decide which idea to follow and manifest, I could really do with some guidance' I told him.

His broad grin matched his sparkly eyes as he placed his arm around my shoulder, making it impossible to feel anything but genuine love and he said, 'Liz, your courage and determination make me smile and you will get the guidance and help you need, we have heard your prayers in Spirit and it is up to you to be open enough, to let go of control and let the magic begin.' I felt my body relax and I smiled, knowing that he was so right about me needing to let go of control.

At that glorious moment a beam of white light appeared in front of us and began to slowly form into a band of many shining Spirit forms. The forms had a gentle and loving feeling, an energy that encompassed my whole being. I was thrown into a pool of peace, of love, of knowing and I heard White Owl's voice in the distance say, 'Meet the Messengers'.

White Owl's voice continued with conviction, 'You are being invited to write about the Messengers and convey their wisdom so that others may find some comfort and solace in the words that you channel. There will be times when you doubt the messages coming through but keep returning your focus, keep praying and this book will have a magic of its own. Are you up to the challenge Liz?' In the loud silence my voice seemed far away but I heard myself say, 'Uh huh'.

I was so in the moment, nothing else existed except peace and unconditional love. One by one the various Messengers introduced themselves and I felt light, amazed, and uplifted. Any doubts I had about writing another book were gone. I realised they were influencing my thoughts and ideas and all I would have to do was make the effort to sit in front of my computer and begin writing. That was my last thought as I fell asleep.

When I awoke the next morning my memory of everything that happened in my special place the previous night was hazy but what I just described was basically how it unfolded. I guess I was in a trance-like dream state as many of us are when we are drifting into sleep.

I felt enthusiastic and began to write. However, it was not as easy as I anticipated. White Owl was correct. I had to deal with my consistent doubt and questioning about the information that came through. Eventually I began to accept that I am merely a messenger for the Messengers and I know you will benefit from their wisdom and care.

The intention for this book is that everyone who uses it will feel peace and some form of comfort. The peace will not be given, as it already lives within you, but the healing vibration of this book may assist in unlocking what already lies within. Let the magic begin!

MEET THE MESSENGERS

Messengers from Spirit come in many forms. In the thirty years that I have worked as a spiritual medium, I have seen and communicated with many. There are spirit guides, angels, archangels, ascended masters, those who have passed over, animal spirits, fairies and even flowers, crystals and plant life can be Messengers of Spirit. My heartfelt understanding is that there is one, beautiful, intelligent all-knowing energy that manifests as a spark of light inherent in all life on Earth. I also believe there are many realms of existence that we are not aware of and that they too are part of the universal tapestry.

Messengers from Spirit are our allies, they are there to assist, guide, impress, heal and comfort. Spirit Guides and allies form a personal support team around each of us during our time here on Earth. Although it seems we are often alone during our time here on Earth, I truly believe we are not. There are limitations including not being allowed to interfere with our power of choice as that is a huge reason why we originally incarnated. Free will is what elevates our souls through the wisdom we gain. It is not imperative that we become consciously aware of our Spirit allies, they will support us regardless.

In whatever form Spirit visits you, they are all guides. At times, Spirit will use archetypal forms that they know you will relate to – this explains why some guides appear as Buddhist monks, tribal elders, nuns, and so on. Their presentation may also be linked to a former lifetime they experienced, possibly where they connected with you.

Shape shifting into different forms is apparently easy to achieve in the Spirit world.

Of course we all want to see them, hear them, talk to them and know more about them. Who are *my* guides, *my* angels, how can they help? As with anything, if we put our time, energy and awareness into conscious communication with the Spirit world, it can be done by any of us. We just have to believe in ourselves and in Spirit and take the steps to make it happen. One of the most effective things we can do to hear Spirit is to simply learn how to be quiet within. A prayer to Spirit goes a long way also. They are always listening; we just have to believe. What we achieve and manifest in this life are often a consequence of wanting something enough. If we want something with a burning passion and are prepared to go the extra distance, we can achieve anything. If you want to communicate with Spirit, if you keep at it, it will happen.

I am still learning and have varying degrees of success from day to day with my personal communication with Spirit. I love it when it is crystal clear but at other times it is like the phone line is engaged or disconnected. At these times we are left with our faith as our guide, knowing they have not deserted us but the communication lines are down for a reason unbeknown to us.

I asked my own personal Spirit Guide, White Owl, who I introduced in my first book, *For the Love of Spirit*, to enlighten us as to how we can best communicate with those in Spirit.

Below is an interview I conducted with White Owl.

INTERVIEW WITH WHITE OWL

Liz

White Owl, how can one communicate with Spirit?

White Owl

There is a place within each of you that you touch on every day in the moments between your thoughts. Your inner radar responds to theses flashes of insight and feelings but your logical mind is like the strict parent who puts down tough boundaries and encourages you to deny your intuition. With practice, you can choose to give these moments more credit and honour. As you begin to shift your faith from the logical to the intuitive and give yourself permission to own your spiritual self, your ability to see, feel and hear Spirit will increase.

Liz

Is there anything we can do to help this process?

White Owl

Have fun, yes, have fun! Humans are forgetting the simple pleasures of being alive. With so many expectations and responsibilities weighing you down it is no wonder. However, you all have the power to choose to approach life with a lighter heart, mind and soul. When the self is light and happy your vibration elevates and it is easier to tap into the subtle vibrations of your higher self and commune with Spirit. It really can be that simple.

Reach out for support from Spirit and from those around you. Many of you feel you have to struggle alone, be proud and weather storms without support. Humans need each other and unless you ask for help, no one will know you need it. There is also a universal law about asking Spirit for help. Spirit cannot intervene without your permission except under specific circumstances. So please, swallow your pride, be like a child and reach out when you are unsure, afraid or alone. Spirit and people respect and love a humble soul and the lesson of humility will aid in your communication with the Spirit world.

Liz

How do we know that the Spiritual Messengers who come to us are genuine and not imposters or negative souls?

White Owl

First of all, you need to understand what *negative souls* or lower realm entities are. Imagine looking at bacteria under a microscope, they are all wriggling around and look most unattractive. Certain bacteria thrive in specific environments. For example, mould will thrive in damp moist environments. However, if you remove the environmental conditions, the bacteria will cease to exist as it cannot survive without the right conditions.

Same with undesired entities, they need a low energy environment; they prefer illness, sadness, depression, and loneliness and are quite partial to drugged or drunken atmospheres.

You will know the energy of Spirit in your heart when it is real. You will feel a sense of wonder and an uplifting feeling. A negative energy is simply that, negative, and you feel it. Even if the lower energy is dressed in angel wings, something will not feel right and it is up to you to trust your own reactions. If you protect yourself each time you go within by asking the angels, surrounding yourself with white light, or whatever method you choose, you should not encounter such low vibrational energies.

If you do encounter a lost soul or an uncomfortable energy simply ask your angels and guides to send it on its way. By doing that you automatically uplift your own vibration and the entity cannot survive in that environment. This may sound simplistic and yes, it is simple. The world has become a complex place where in origin, life is simple and so is the Spirit world.

You can also talk aloud to the entity coming from a place of love, not fear, and ask them to look for the light. You can burn sage sticks, burn essential oils, say prayers and play uplifting music. Create an environment of love where only joy and peace can exist.

Liz

So basically, White Owl, we have to honour those quiet moments, our insights and gut feelings and naturally we will be able to hear and sense those in Spirit? It also helps to create a safe and sacred space and be conscious to protect ourselves spiritually. Is there anything else we can do to open our communication with Spirit?

White Owl

Meditation is another activity to heighten Spirit communication, but keep it simple. Perhaps watch a sunrise instead of television, lay on the grass or sand once in a while, and notice the crispness of the air on a cool day, or the colour of the rose petals. These are all forms of meditation. Certainly sitting cross-legged and closing your eyes for an hour is also beneficial but experiment with what brings you a sense of peace. Meditation should not be difficult or uncomfortable. It is a natural human state that has been somewhat forgotten.

Simply talk to your Spirit friends either mentally, aloud or through journaling. We do hear you and we will respond in the best way we possibly can. Be patient and build a relationship with us, just as you would if you had just met someone new on Earth. It takes time for us to align our energy with your personal vibration. Once that is achieved, conscious communication is more consistent. We prefer that this process be subtle, over time, as to do it too quickly may cause a level of discomfort.

Even though we may feel invisible to you, have faith, keep communicating and enjoy the unfoldment of discovering us, as we will with you. We are so proud of each and every one of you for taking on this life you are leading which we understand is challenging and daunting at times. Life never ends even when the body expires but remember to honour the present moment and that the life you have now is a precious gem in a vast and mystical universe.

Liz

What about the times when we do all the right things like meditate and try to hear your guidance, but we are met with silence?

There are many complexities why this may occur. Some of them include:

- When you are feeling stress and worry, your vibration is low, and your auric field contracted. It is like having a weak Wi-Fi signal when it takes a long time for anything to download. We suggest you focus on prayer and we will find another way to answer you, such as in a dream or with a sign.
- You are hearing us but you are not believing it or only hearing what you want to hear.
- It's our day off, (White Owl roars with laughter) just joking.
- There are certain conditions and circumstances where we are not permitted to intervene.
- We may not be aligned enough at that time with your vibration and the communication is temporarily down.

There are other reasons that may be tailor-made to your individual circumstances.

Remember to be patient, to slow down the mind and uplift your vibration, if possible. Never for a moment think that we are ignoring you. Sometimes, for a child to learn, the parent has to step back and not interfere. The child knows the parent is there in the background which gives them the confidence to explore and make mistakes, so that greater learning can occur. We are like that parent; we are watching out for you but there are times it is best we hold back. This is where trust and faith, not only in us but in your own self, are of upmost importance.

DEFINITIONS

Spirit wants to talk to you in the pages ahead. This book is a gift to you from Spirit. It is a tool for your journey that you can pick up again and again when you feel you need some guidance, help or comfort.

Here are some of my personal definitions, feelings and insights of some of the Messengers you will meet in the pages ahead.

Spirit Guides

Spirit Guides have lived on the Earth before and they have a good knowledge of the earthly plane along with all its possibilities and limitations. Often they have not incarnated into a physical body for some time and have ascended their vibration in the Spirit World. They have a karmic bond to you and are eager to assist you in any way they can. They cannot influence your free will but they can nudge, suggest, and steer you – just as a parent can with their teenager. Spirit Guides often impress upon me a wonderful sense of humour. Because they have lived on Earth at some point, they appreciate that humour is an uplifting tool to which we can relate.

We all have one or two main guides from birth to death. We also have other guides who come and go at different times in our lives, depending on what we are going through. For example, if you were learning how to sing, a singing guide may journey alongside of you for a time. Once, when I was experiencing a difficult relationship break-up, I was sent a guide in the form of an earthly psychologist. I was told his energy would be able to help me find my way on those darker days when I felt hurt and alone. Spirit Guides can impress you with thoughts that can be solutions to problems, or they can send you signs – although you have to be open and receptive to recognising them.

While writing this book, I met many different Spirit Guides who were not necessarily *mine*. They were drawn to helping me with this book and it is likely that I will not see some of them again. They had a service to do by participating in this project.

Spirit Guides love you and want to help you. Ask for their help. Once you have asked, as White Owl pointed out, do know that they have heard you and be patient with their response.

Ascended Masters

Ascended Masters are those souls who have lived on Earth and made a mark in our history books. We still look to them for guidance and comfort. Some examples are Jesus, Buddha, Mother Theresa, Gandhi and, who knows, maybe even John F Kennedy, John Lennon and Marilyn Monroe! My interpretation of an Ascended Master is a wise soul now residing in Spirit who has lived and breathed our earthly air. When they were on Earth they learned well and left us something to think about or aspire to.

I love working with Ascended Masters. Their vibration is elevated and when you connect with them you feel a natural high. They are powerful allies. You can receive their help by focusing on them and sincerely asking for their guidance.

Angels and Archangels

Angels feel like a deep breath of fresh air in a cool green forest. They breathe light and love into dark corners of our hearts and minds. They can break rules and do the impossible when they know it is beneficial and right to do so. I have no doubt that angels exist and if you don't believe in angels, which is totally acceptable, try asking them to prove they are with you and I have absolutely no doubt they will. Some people believe angels have never lived an earthly life and perhaps they have not, I am not completely sure. I am more inclined to believe that they can make and break rules where needed.

I sense when angels are near and occasionally I hear their words. Several times I have heard angels singing and it is an exquisite sound. They are incredible healers in terms of shifting undesirable energy that is within us and around us. Their compassion knows no limits and they will support you and bring out the best in you for you to examine and accept.

Every time I have seen Archangels, they seem rather tall. Archangels are specialty angels overlooking a specific life area. There are personal guardian angels, romance angels, healing angels and, of course, we all love the car parking angels! Angels respond to prayers swiftly, and my sense is that there is an abundance of angels and enough for each and every one of us.

Angels reside on a fine and subtle vibration but they can be accessed if you are patient and can train yourself to be quiet enough inside yourself to feel them. I sense we are constantly graced by their presence, regardless of our awareness of them. If we are lucky, there may be moments in our lives when we see or feel them spontaneously. I treasure those moments. They have graced us all by visiting the pages of this book. Look out for them between the lines.

People Who Have Passed Over

Standing on my balcony one sunny morning, I was wretched with worry. I paced up and down wringing my hands. I was so concerned about my 20-year-old son that day, and I wanted a sign from Spirit to show me what I could do to help him, but I could not penetrate the walls of silence between myself and Spirit. Suddenly, I heard the voice of my deceased father in my head say very clearly, *This kid needs to be self-employed and he needs to start young.* It rang so true and felt so real that, after that message, my husband and I helped him start his own business. It worked well for some time and was instrumental in forming his young adult years.

When I was heavily pregnant with my second child, I had an anxiety attack one evening when I was alone as I was allowing negative thoughts to take over. *What if something is wrong with the baby? What if something goes wrong with the birth?* Amidst my turmoil I suddenly felt the calm presence of two people beside me. When I closed my eyes I saw my grandmother in Spirit on one side and my grandfather in Spirit on the other, both holding me. Without one word being spoken, I felt totally reassured. They embraced me in a calm aura of love and peace. I breathed in those precious moments and knew that my baby would be fine. My son was born perfect and the birth went well, proving my fears to be unfounded.

Those who love us do not stop loving us when they pass over. Although they transcend to a new life, the cords of true love can never be broken. Our loved ones in Spirit take great joy in helping us any way they can.

If you receive a message in this book from a Messenger that reminds you of one of your loved ones in Spirit, it may well be them guiding you to that particular message. For example, if you received the message from the Messenger Butterfly and your now-deceased mother told you she would send you butterflies when she passed over, it may be her sending you that specific message. Trust your intuition when interpreting the messages that resonate with you and your life. It is also possible that only one thing rings true in any given message and this is where you can use your own intuition and extract the guidance that is your gift.

Animal Spirits

When animals, including our beloved pets, pass over they are welcomed into the Spirit realm just as we are. I have often seen and communicated with animals in Spirit when doing medium readings for others. I find it interesting that I hear the animal Spirits speak in words using the English language, but there is so much we do not understand about the other side. I assume the priority is getting a legible message through to the medium and Spirit will use any tools available to make that happen.

Animals Spirits can act as guides by impressing their energy and unique gifts upon our energy field. If you were facing a challenge where you needed extra courage, you could call on the vibration of the lion or perhaps you will get a sign of a lion in the form of an image on television, or hear a song on the radio.

While demonstrating mediumship in a class I was teaching, I clairvoyantly saw a red robin, flying around the classroom. The cute bird would land on the shoulder of a student and let me know the message that was coming through was for that person. Earlier in the day, we had been learning about animal spirits and the energy we had built up in the classroom seemed to welcome the little bird. He, or perhaps she, was acting as my personal assistant during the demonstration and it was incredibly uplifting and delightful.

Many indigenous cultures have been aware of the power of animal spirits for eons and you can research this online for more insight about animal spirits and their meanings.

While writing this book, I felt some powerful animal spirits come forward and I felt honoured. You will meet some of them in your personal messages.

Fairies, Nature and Flowers

Fairies and nature spirits come on a vibration that is lively, playful, and exciting. They are close to the Earth, yet are very connected to Spirit. They have a balance of earthly and heavenly energies in their makeup. They are great manifesters, healers and environmentalists! They encourage us to look after Mother Earth and the environment.

There are tall fairies, small flower fairies and all sorts of nature spirits that can present in many forms.

One evening I saw a fairy face superimposed on a poorly maintained bottlebrush tree. I was dining in the outdoor area of a restaurant with my family. There was a beautiful sunset unfolding and as I looked out to the horizon, admiring the gold and orange sky, my attention was drawn to a nearby neglected tree.

A translucent face with tear-drop eyes framed with golden hair appeared clearly over the tree. The apparition lasted for around a minute as I squinted to see if I was hallucinating. The feeling coming from the fairy was one of sadness and I intuitively knew it was because the tree had not been well-cared-for and was dying. Several months later I drove past the restaurant and noticed the tree had been removed.

Fairies are active everywhere in nature and I believe each flower has a fairy, so every time you place flowers in a vase you are placing fairies in your house. The fairies will remain as long as the flowers have life and the same for plants.

I have always found their intentions are to be helpful and they are happy to listen to your requests for guidance and help.

Writing this book, I was graced with several fairies, particularly when I spent time outdoors to receive the messages.

Flowers are powerful allies that we tend to overlook in our daily lives. When there is a special occasion, such as a wedding, we think flowers. When someone is ill or passed over, we think flowers. When we are in love, we think flowers. Flowers are powerful yet humble; they are powerful healers and messengers and they bring light where there is darkness.

Recently there was a tragic event where many people perished. On the news report, I saw a mountain of flowers that people had brought to the scene to honour those who had passed. The energy of the flowers was not only honouring those who had died but was clearing the environment and comforting those experiencing loss and grief. The flowers were eventually taken to be composted and put on a shrine as an additional tribute to the victims. The power of flowers is deeper than we yet realise.

You can benefit from flower energy by accessing them in the fresh form, as an image, in a flower essence or in an essential oil. I place flower images on my screen saver when I sense I could benefit from their specific healing properties.

Flowers are servants of the divine and here to uplift you, so enjoy them, embrace them, see them as significant messengers in your life, and connect to them intuitively.

The Visions

While channelling the messages from Spirit in this book, I was shown a vision as each Messenger appeared – which I briefly describe at the beginning of each message. I wanted to share these visions with you not only so you could know what I was experiencing but because the vision may mean something to you personally. If you feel to, meditate upon the vision and ask Spirit for further guidance.

The Lesson

After each message was conveyed to me, the Messenger explained that the lesson associated with the message would give more meaning and depth to you, the inquirer. Read the lesson and sit with it. What does it mean for you personally? How else could you view the situation you are inquiring about? Look for the *bigger picture* meaning.

Power Choice

I have included the section Power Choice to empower you, the inquirer. I believe we are never victims of circumstance; choice is our powerful sword that can turn our lives around or turn them upside down! We will do both at one time or another as we are human and we are here to learn. Not all of us have been guided to use our power of choice wisely; I certainly feel I was never taught to and I continue to learn about choice all the time.

The Power Choice mentioned in each message is further guidance from Spirit but you may have even more appropriate ideas that are right for you, follow them and, again, trust your intuition!

Your body is housing a powerhouse called your soul – feel it, love it and let it explore and grow!

Affirmation

There is an affirmation included at the end of each message as inspiration to help you on your journey. I have found affirmations to be a powerful tool on my journey of growth and development. Affirmations can be said, thought, written, sung or yelled. Focusing on positive words and thoughts is a healing process that can bring immense rewards. You may prefer to create your own affirmations that relate to the messages.

Momentary Meditations

This section was inspired by Spirit half-way through writing the book. White Owl asked me to include it with each message to inspire you to feel empowered about whatever you are going through at present. White Owl explained that since the internet and mobile phones have dominated many of our lifestyles, our attention spans have become shorter and more difficult to focus. We are being bombarded with so much information that our minds are often spinning and out of synch with our true selves.

Short, regular meditations are powerful and help to harness the mind, without threatening it too much. Even though some of the momentary meditations are less than one-minute-long, they will give you a lift. White Owl said he has blessed each meditation with his sacred sage stick and you will feel a quiet power and healing when doing them.

Liz's Comments

As I progressed further into writing this book, I felt guided to add more information from my own personal insights, which are often peppered by White Owl's opinions. I sensed that Spirit felt this would make the book more complete and give you valuable understandings into whatever challenges you currently face. I often describe my own life situations to illustrate a point made in the message. I believe we are all here in the same boat, none of us are above one another, and none of us below. It is important to support and understand each other with as much unconditional love as we can muster. Sharing and communicating honestly and openly is a wonderful way to connect with each other.

HOW TO USE THIS BOOK

Creating Intention

You will receive a more accurate message if you take a moment to set your intention for receiving the message or messages that are most appropriate for you.

I suggest that you firstly clear the energy of the book by:

- Knocking on the book and then using your thumb to roll through the pages. Knocking will shake old energy out and touching each page will absorb your personal energy, or
- Using a sage smudge stick to clear the energy. Wave the smoke around the book while focusing and seeing the book cleansed and full of light, or
- Holding the book, close your eyes and visualise yourself breathing white light in and out. On the out breath, blow on the book with the intention of cleansing. Breath is a powerful cleanser.
- When the book is not being used, leave an amethyst crystal (or any crystal you prefer to use for cleansing and protection) on it. This will maintain uplifting vibrations and protection from undesirable energy.

Ask a Question

Once the book has been cleared, you are now ready to give yourself a reading.

I recommend holding the book close to your heart while sincerely asking for help with a specific issue or for a general reading. If you are sincere and open to hearing whatever Spirit wants you to hear, you will get a more accurate result.

You can then:

- Simply open the book randomly and read the message that appears.
- Choose a number from one to fifty, as there are fifty messages. This method is recommended for kindle readers.
- Choose more than one message, if you wish, just as you would with tarot or angel cards. If the first message feels incomplete, repeat the process taking note of the previous messages and how they connect.

Trust your own intuition when receiving the messages as to how they apply to your unique situation.

Thank Spirit and be aware of any repetitive thoughts, feelings or signs that occur after your reading. Spirit will continue to help you after your message has been read.

Thank the Messenger, thank Spirit. Be aware of the energy of the Messenger who came to you in the reading. That Messenger may bring you signs throughout the coming day or week to let you know you are not alone and that Spirit has heard your prayers.

I have faith in you. I have faith in Spirit that whatever challenges you now face can be seen through eyes of gratitude, understanding, and unconditional love. We are all in this together as we are all part of each other. Remember to reach out to those who love you here on Earth and in Spirit.

Enjoy your gifts of guidance!

The Messages

MESSAGE 1

❖

Love One Another

Messenger

Angel of Compassion

Happiness can exist only in acceptance.
– George Orwell

Vision

An angel tending to bright-pink roses that cover a garden fence.

Message

The Angel of Compassion and the pink roses radiate the energy of unconditional love, perseverance, and steadfastness.

Tolerance of those around you is advised at this time.

Assuming that we understand another's predicament is easy to do, yet remember that only the individual in question and the universe know the truth.

Our unique relationship to the universe is sacred and often unspoken. Spirit asks you to consider the saying, *Be kind as every person is fighting their own battle.*

We cannot change people but we can change how we respond to them. Someone around you may be processing some intense issues. Take a step back and allow them time and space. Trying to *fix* things for them is not advised.

By pulling your energy in and focusing on your own processes, a stronger relationship can prevail with those you care about.

If you find yourself particularly tired of late, you may be unconsciously giving your power away to others. We all do this at times by allowing another's energy to inadvertently invade our own.

Dance the dance that is yours, not someone else's.

Breathe easy, relax and let go.

Lesson

Developing compassion, giving others room to explore their own strengths and weaknesses.

Power Choices

- Avoid gossip.
- Be selective who you spend time with.
- Spending time alone now is beneficial to your soul growth.
- Call on Spirit to assist with releasing attachment to desired outcomes.

Momentary Meditation

Imagine you are in a botanical garden. You become aware of a picket fence covered in bright-pink roses. You see an angel watering the roses. The angel holds out her hand offering a pink rose to you, which you accept. As you touch the rose, a bolt of loving healing fills your heart and soul. Healing has taken place; it is done, and it is so.

Affirmation

I lovingly accept people for who they are.

Liz's Comments

This message reminds me how easy it is to get caught up in other people's vortexes, particularly those we love. It can be heart-wrenching to watch our loved ones battle their own demons and, at times, fail. We are more useful when we remain in our own power while offering love, support, and compassion from an optimistic standpoint. There are also times when the best thing we can do is to give a person space.

My children have been my biggest teachers when it comes to learning to accept people for who they are, particularly now that they have become young adults. Parenting may well be the biggest teacher of unconditional love.

They are beautiful human beings and because I love them dearly, I must totally accept them for who they are – including the choices they make, even though there are times I don't agree with their decisions.

Forcing issues often ends in frustration and when we let go of outcomes, things tend to fall into place.

Take heart, the universe really is on your side and advises self-preservation at this time.

MESSAGE 2

Taking Care of Business

Messenger

Archangel Metatron

Action is the foundational key to all success.
– Picasso

Vision

A graceful angel's hand organises colourful building blocks into order and structure.

Message

Love and laughter can permeate your life when you feel centred and have attended to business.

What commitments have you been avoiding? Perhaps it is doing something loving for yourself, such as making positive food choices, finishing a project, decluttering your environment or clearing financial debts. Acts such as these induce positive energy, allowing more room in your life and mind to clearly see options and opportunities in front of you.

Archangel Metatron wants you to know that magic is possible in any area of life but the laws of the universe say you must act responsibly and deal with whatever you may be avoiding before optimum forward movement is possible.

If you asked a specific question today, the answer is to consider taking a down-to-earth approach. In what way could you view your current situation from a practical point of view? The answer lies in taking positive and effective action.

Lesson

Accountability, attending to business.

Power Choice

- Make an honest self-appraisal of what business needs attending to in your life.
- Do not hesitate to seek professional help if required from an accountant, a counsellor or life coach.
- Delegate tasks, if appropriate.
- Write a to-do-list.
- Include Archangel Metatron in your requests for assistance.

Momentary Meditation

Sitting comfortably, place your focus on your feet. Imagine and sense tree roots growing from the soles of your feet into Mother Earth beneath you. Feel yourself becoming grounded and connected in your body and to the Earth. Once you are relaxed, ask Archangel Metatron for assistance and any further messages. Be aware of flashes of insight and new ideas. This is often the way Spirit communicates with us.

Affirmation

There is clarity and joy in all that I do.

Liz's Comments

This message reminds us of our own power and encourages us to activate the power of choice. When we feel *stuck* in our lives, we experience indecision. The state of mind accompanying indecision is often more uncomfortable than taking action, even when one is not certain what action to pursue.

Even the most organised person has moments of procrastination and conscious delay. Perhaps it is a human trait or maybe we just avoid certain tasks because they are plain boring! Such is the way of the earth realm we live in; it demands that we find balance in doing, being, and feeling.

Sitting here now, I spy the accounting books for my business that need updating by four months.

From my experience, making a plan does help. A goal without a plan often doesn't eventuate. There is also wisdom in taking small steps by breaking things down into achievable goals.

I could choose to plan to get my accounting books in order in the next month. I could plan and commit to completing one month of accounts each week. Then I could break it down to five minutes a day for the next month. Task complete!

It is also interesting to note that decluttering is a powerful form of modern-day alchemy. If you feel emotionally challenged at present, declutter your bathroom. For career issues, declutter the living area. For health issues, declutter the kitchen. For romance to improve, declutter the bedroom. If childhood issues are holding you back, declutter the attic, garage or basement. Whether you choose to declutter one drawer or the whole room, an impact will be felt. I have successfully applied this approach many times.

This concept can also be applied to our devices by deleting old emails and text messages allowing room for forward movement.

Archangel Metatron is known for his ability to assist with prioritising and is eager to support you at this time.

MESSAGE 3

Light

Messenger

The Sun

If light is in your heart, you will find your way home.
– Rumi

Vision

Sunlight streaming through a dark forest.

Message

It is time to open your heart to the light, to see the light in yourself and the world around you. We have a choice to count our blessings or to focus on what is not right in ourselves and in our lives. Gratitude is a quiet power that we have only begun to discover.

In this moment, consider one positive attribute about yourself. Send love and gratitude to that quality. Then name another quality you love about yourself. You will soon become aware of many of your inner gifts.

Focus on a situation that is bothering you right now. Within each shadow is a gift. Are you learning wisdom, patience, or perhaps being honest with yourself and others?

The light is here to help you, simply by acknowledging its existence. Darkness is but an illusion as when light appears, darkness vanishes.

The light and truth will now shine on whatever concerns you today. Face whatever is challenging you. Look for the silver lining, and clarity shall be yours.

Lesson

Awareness and acceptance of the light within.

Power Choice

- Open the curtains to allow the light in.
- Burn candles.
- Breathe in light.
- Spend time in the sun.
- Focus on gratitude.

Momentary Meditation

Inhale deeply while visualising light entering your lungs. Hold this light in for a few seconds and then exhale darkness, making room for the light. You can now breathe in light easily and gently.

Affirmation

I am the light.

Liz's Comments

This message asks us to release superficial judgements of ourselves and situations we are in. It encourages us to search deeper in our hearts, rather than accept everything our minds tells us as the truth. Now is an opportunity to ascend to a higher level of understanding.

In moments of meditation throughout my life, there have been some special moments where I completely became one with light. Once, as a teenager, I was innocently walking to the laundromat when, for five random seconds, I was above my body, watching it walk down the street. Those five seconds altered my whole outlook on life as I merged with a light and power that encompassed me in complete peace.

More recently, I had an outer-body experience during a meditation. I found myself hovering over Planet Earth and was totally in love with every square metre of it. No judgement or fear. I just felt unconditional love. Perhaps you have had a similar experience.

Although fleeting, in those timeless moments I became one with everything. I knew everything there was to know. I sense this is what death is like, being one with the light and able to be in an endless moment of unconditional love. There is a part within us that is connected to each other and all things.

We often feel separated from *source* in human form, but the light within us is consistent and accessible. We can call on our angels, helpers, and guides to assist with our sense of connection to source.

Spirit can help us when we make a conscious effort to focus on the light and on our inner selves. Such is the importance of spending time within and seeking balance and harmony in our lives.

MESSAGE 4

Standing Tall

Messenger

The Tiger

All our dreams can come true,
if we have the courage to pursue them.
– Walt Disney

Vision

A magnificent tiger perched on a mountain ledge, roaring loudly.

Message

Great strength and bravery come to you now in the form of the Spirit of the Tiger.

You can now cut through stubborn energy that has previously held you back. Be aware of opportunities, they may arrive unexpectedly, so be ready to pounce. Deep within you, there has been a significant shift which is allowing new energy to present itself in the form of potential prospects. You have many angels of support cheering you on.

As daybreak gives relief from a dark night, your life is now lightening up. Whatever disagreements, conflicts and disharmony have been in your life recently regarding relationships, specific situations or within yourself, it is time to move forward.

Clarity can now be gained by paying attention to your gut feelings rather than logic. Your challenge is to listen to your inner ally, your own inner guidance system. This will ensure you are in the right places at the right time.

Release any resentments and negative feelings that act as a barrier to your progress. Remember, you are more powerful than you realise. Know that you are completely protected and safe as you make this wonderful transition of moving forward.

Lesson

Accepting your own power.

Power Choice

- Stand tall and have confidence.
- Avoid naysayers and fear-based consciousness.
- Allow qualities of bravery to emerge.
- Call on the Spirit of the Tiger.

Momentary Meditation

Imagine you are on a cliff, overlooking a beautiful blue ocean. You confidently jump off the cliff and feel the exhilaration and joy as you fall gently into the ocean below. You feel empowered, strong, and competent.

Affirmation

I am powerful and capable; I trust my inner guidance.

Liz's Comments

Sometimes life calls on us to be brave. Bravery is a loaded emotion which can bring up feelings of inadequacy and fear. It also brings to the surface a primal rush of adrenalin and feelings of excitement.

Bravery is also linked, on a deep level, to our innate wisdom and intuition. How many true stories have we heard of a hero having a *feeling* or a *knowing* that they had to go somewhere at a certain time or to check on someone they loved?

I was walking my dog when I had a clear intuitive thought suggesting I walk down a particular street. Even though it was out of my way, I chose to obey the thought, reasoning that the extra walk would be good exercise for me and my beloved dog, Charlie.

As I turned the corner of the street, a man lay on the footpath unconscious with a head injury. There was no-one else around. Of course, I called an ambulance and then totally understood why I had had that intuitive thought.

For many years, I had a desire to write a column in a newspaper. I had no real experience. I eventually summoned the courage to send an email to the editor of a local newspaper offering to do an angel/psychic column. To my utter amazement, I received an email saying they were open to the idea and asking me to come in and see them. My column began the following month.

I wrote that column for twelve months and connected with some lovely people in the process. It was a great learning curve and something I could do while my children were still young. Not long after that, I gained the confidence to write my first book.

When we take a leap outside our comfort zones, the universe can happily deliver opportunities. It is then up to us to be brave enough to accept the challenge on offer and to align our bravery and our gut feelings.

The message today is to be brave, go outside your comfort zone and accept the gifts on offer.

MESSAGE 5

—•※•—

Honouring Your Needs

Messenger

Archangel Raphael

You yourself, as much as anybody in the entire universe,
deserve your love and affection.
– Buddha

Vision

A tall angel, dressed in an emerald green cape, standing on water.

Message

You have been putting out a great deal of energy and it is now time
to reel in your energy and feel the calm.

This can happen simply by opening up to nature and all of its
beauty or perhaps spending time with those who uplift you. Simple
pleasures bring huge rewards to the body, mind, and spirit. Now is

a time for rewarding yourself and making choices that please you. This is neither selfish nor vain, it is self-love.

It is wise to incorporate these activities into your life regularly to create a healthy balance. We can compare our existence to a pyramid. Our bodies and basic well-being are represented by the base of the pyramid, our emotions the middle and our spiritual selves the pinnacle. The base holds the others up.

Archangel Raphael, the healing angel, encourages you to seek his help through simply asking. Any niggling health issues that have been an issue of late will soon disappear when you give permission to your body, mind, and soul to relax.

At times, we tend to be our own worst enemies and this message is a reminder to avoid creating unrealistic demands on yourself.

Alternatively, this message may be regarding emotional health. If you have been overwhelmed with intense feelings, Spirit advises taking time out to process them through gentle activities that bring you a sense of peace.

Pace your life to a rhythm that sits comfortably with your body, mind, and spirit.

Lesson

Adjusting your pace of life to your own rhythm.

Power Choice

- Review your daily itinerary and make changes that promote balance in your life.
- Consume foods that give you energy.
- Choose gentle exercise that is meditative and relaxing.
- Give yourself permission to nap and daydream.
- Read books that are inspiring.
- Spend time at a spa or retreat.

Momentary Meditation

Visualise a spiral of emerald-green healing light descending over your body from your head down. Feel its calm and nurturing healing energy. Breathe in the green light to your heart and gently release.

Affirmation

I am healthy and calm and balanced. All is well.

Liz's Comments

Healing is simply about balance. When we are not in balance, our bodies and our moods will try to communicate that something is out of synch. We live in a busy, demanding world but often we feel guilty if we take time out for ourselves.

Healing can take place in miraculous ways when we still ourselves within. Realisations and inner guidance from our higher selves and Spirit can flow when we are in a receptive mode and quite simply, become quiet. This is why the expression *sleep on it* is accurate.

When our minds relax, deeper wisdom can come to the surface. When we relax, it allows us to hand our problems over to a higher power, and to have faith that the healing and assistance we need will arrive, as long as we are prepared to do our part.

Where in your life are you stretching yourself to the point of discomfort? How can self-care strategies help balance this situation? It may be as simple as asking for support or allowing yourself a day off from your usual activities. Honour your needs and watch new seeds sprout.

While editing this book, I needed a break as all the words were looking the same. I lay on the couch in the middle of the day and watched utter nonsense on cable television. Not a spiritual or uplifting activity, yet it was perfect, as I needed something contrary after focusing on the spiritual content of the book.

After an hour, I was re-energised and came back to the book. Allow yourself do whatever it is you need to do to find balance.

MESSAGE 6

—•※•—

Happiness

Messenger

Lavender Fairies

Be happy for this moment. This moment is your life.
— Omar Khayyam

Vision

Joyful, purple fairies, dancing in fields of lavender.

Message

Happiness arrives in moments. Happiness is not something that we one day receive, such as a dream job, the perfect relationship, a house or a great body.

Happiness surprises us when we least expect it. It may arrive in a smile from a stranger, a laugh between friends or a butterfly dancing before your eyes. Happiness may be an epiphany in the shower, or feelings of upliftment while strolling through a park.

The Lavender Fairies are putting you on notice to be aware of special moments coming in around you, and to be ready to embrace vibrations of happiness, creating a ripple effect of joy in your life.

Whatever challenges you currently face, have faith in your powers of manifestation. Spirit is advising that through plugging into the vibration of happiness and uplifting your spirit, you will naturally attract whatever it is you need to enable you to go forward.

Worrying about a current situation is blocking the answers you seek. Put the worry aside, at least temporarily, and focus on what is wonderful in life, and solutions will appear.

Lesson

Accepting that you are worthy of true happiness.

Power Choice

- Bring lavender flowers or photographs of lavender into your environment.
- Use lavender oil as a perfume or in an oil burner.
- Wear lavender-coloured clothes.
- Focus on special moments and anything that uplifts your soul.
- Write a gratitude list.

Momentary Meditation

Imagine you are strolling through a field of endless lavender flowers. The scent is delicious and calming. With each step you feel an overwhelming sense of peace descending upon you.

Affirmation

I deserve and accept happiness.

Liz's Comments

This message reminds us to re-evaluate what happiness means to us. The media tell us we need a better car, a perfect body, a better house or a perfect relationship to be happy. It's easy to forget that simplicity is loaded with happy moments.

In the past, I worked as a nursing assistant to the elderly. It was an invaluable experience and I loved connecting with the elderly residents. A lovely lady, Mary, (not her real name) said to me one day, 'If I could turn back time, I would grow flowers, all sorts of lovely colourful flowers, as flowers always give me much joy.' I asked Mary, 'Is there any reason you didn't?' 'Oh, I never had time, and when I retired I was ill so it never eventuated,' Mary replied. I mentioned this conversation to her family the next time they visited. The following week they arrived with some lovely potted flower seedlings and placed them in Mary's courtyard. Mary gained great pleasure from nurturing them and watching them grow.

Although Mary's regret was not earth-shattering, it helped me realise how I can dismiss simple pleasures as not worth investing time or energy into, setting myself up to miss out on joy.

Every day is one we will never get back so it makes sense to fill our days with as much joy as possible. Not all days are filled with major life events like getting the perfect job, travelling to exotic locations, meeting our soul mate or having a child. In between, life can be repetitive and, at times, boring.

Our power lies in simple moments, making simple choices that bring joy to ourselves and, in the process, illuminating the world around us.

MESSAGE 7

Hidden Heart

Messenger

Spirit of the Wind

What are you hiding? Is it something from others, or from yourself?
Find your truth. The more you show up, the more you'll be found.
— Brittany Burgunder

Vision

Leaves swirling and dancing in the wind.

Message

Below the surface of each of us lies a factory of feelings being manufactured in response to each experience we have.

Some of these feelings are put aside for processing; others go unnoticed, while others are immediately expressed.

The Spirit of the Wind brings the message that it is time to honour and value the *unnoticed emotions* and to breathe fresh air into the corners of your heart. As each feeling releases, more room will be available for your innate inner wisdom to rise to the surface.

Exciting new research is now suggesting that our heart has similar matter to our brain and the heart may have its own intelligence. By not acknowledging our true heart feelings, it makes sense that we can feel unbalanced and out of sorts.

Feeling harmony between our thoughts and feelings allows our being to experience peace, as the heart and mind are in synch. This requires giving ourselves space to contemplate and arrive at an honest self-appraisal.

Emotions, whether pleasant or uncomfortable, serve as an opportunity for our hearts and souls to blossom and grow. See this time as one of opportunity for emotional balancing and healing past wounds.

If you have asked a specific question today, this message is asking you to look deep within and own your truth.

Lesson

Opening and refreshing the heart centre.

Power Choice

- Ask yourself the question – What area of my life seems blocked or slow? Recall any past events that are connected to this area.

- Focus on your feelings rather than the events.
- Engage in emotional detox activities such as forgiveness meditation, journaling your true feelings, seeing a counsellor or sharing with someone you trust.
- Ask Spirit to guide you to the appropriate method of healing, whether it is from a healer, plant medicine, message or dream.

Momentary Meditation

With a quiet mind, take one hand and place it gently over your heart and breathe. Say the affirmation below several times.

Affirmation

I accept all of my emotions as wonderful teachers in my life.

Liz's Comments

We all deal with our emotions differently due to our individual natures, our upbringing, our cultural values, and influential role models. Personally, the combination of these factors has often found me avoid conflicting emotions, finding them too confrontational for my sensitive self.

When I studied counselling, I learnt that we can heal emotions simply by *putting them on the table* and having a good look at them. It is not weak or shameful to feel anger, sadness, dismay or hurt. I was raised to believe one should carry on regardless of feelings. Therefore, a huge lesson for me, that I am still mastering, is giving myself permission to *feel*. (Having a Virgo moon has also been challenging!)

In my twenties, I was angry with a friend as I felt somewhat neglected and disappointed by her behaviour. I didn't say anything as I simply didn't know how. One day she said to me 'You are really angry with me aren't you?' I quickly denied it. She continued, 'I had a dream that you were furious with me and I woke up knowing it was true'.

I felt so confronted and put on the spot that I admitted she was correct. We had a great conversation and sorted some of our misunderstandings and she was not upset with me for being angry, as I assumed she would be. I need not have put myself through the discomfort. I was blessed she had the dream and that she was tuned into her intuition.

What are you feeling right now that is either not being acknowledged or expressed? It may be the key you need to unlock your movement forward. Clear the air in your heart and the peace you seek will be yours.

MESSAGE 8

·❊·

Grace

Messenger

Great Spirit

Amazing Grace, how sweet the sound …
– John Newton

Vision

A vast spray of sparkling stars, lighting up a dark sky.

Message

The grace of Great Spirit is a powerful gift. Whatever is happening in your life at present is divinely orchestrated. Although free will is powerful, there are times when Great Spirit can override all to bestow gifts of divine intervention. This is such a time.

In Hindu mythology, Gods sometimes granted their devotees *boons*. A boon is when a request from the devotee could be granted by the Gods, even if it meant overriding the laws of karma.

Most of us have bargained with the universe at some point. Now is a time your wishes can be granted with nothing expected in return. It is your time for your boon! Significant astrological alignments presently support this special time and may only happen a few times in any lifetime.

Your challenge now is to be in receptive mode, to know that you certainly are worthy of what the universe wants to bestow upon you. Open your arms, your heart, and your energy field to what is rightfully yours and radiate faith and thanks to the powers that be.

The path ahead is opening up and transporting you to places you cannot yet imagine. There is a part of you that is ready to grow and the universe is answering your call.

Things you have repeatedly asked for in the past may now manifest. Divine timing is at work in your life, open your arms to receive. You are loved and cherished more than you know.

Lesson

Believing in miracles.

Power Choice

- Be open to change.
- Turn your worries into prayers.
- Let go of control.
- Think big.
- Be aware of intuitive dreams.

Momentary Meditation

Imagine you are lying on soft grass on a warm evening, gazing at the stars above. You see a falling star and make a wish.

Affirmation

I am divinely cared for at all times.

Liz's Comments

I loved receiving this message. The vision I experienced was spectacular. In my mind's eye, I saw a million stars brightly lighting up the sky, not unlike the cover of this book. Simultaneously, I downloaded the message as a feeling. We all experience this gift of clair-cognizance at times, where we know something without knowing why we do.

This message reminds me of a bird in a cage. Someone opens the cage door but the bird does not move due to fear and disbelief. You are the bird and the universe is about to open your cage so you can expand, grow, and receive so much more than you can imagine. Your challenge is to leave the cage and have faith that the support and love you need will be available.

Little will change in our lives unless we are prepared to do things differently and this choice often involves elements of risk. Perhaps risk of failure or risk of being hurt.

When I met my second husband he was leaving to work interstate. Before he left he asked me to rent a home for us for when he returned.

Being a surfer, he joked that a home right on the beach would be perfect, which we both laughed about.

An incredible rental property with amazing ocean views fell into my lap within a week. It was expensive and a financial risk, and yet it felt like a gift from the universe. As it was a large home, I was able to run workshops and share the beauty of the home with others. I also conceived my second child there. It was a special time in our lives. We lived there happily for a few years and somehow, the rent always got paid.

What special gifts does Spirit have in store for you? How exciting, enjoy your gifts!

MESSAGE 9

---·❈·---

Trusting the Way Forward

Messenger

Mermaids

Trust in dreams, for in them is hidden the gate to eternity.
– Kahlil Gibran

Vision

A beautiful sunrise lights up the ocean, revealing mermaids playing in the waves.

Message

Mermaids are here to guide you through unknown territory. If you cannot see the outcome to a perplexing situation in your life, compassion and understanding are now bestowed upon you. Mermaids know their way around the deep mysterious ocean and are excellent navigators.

Regardless of seemingly stubborn blocks at present, the Mermaids ask you to maintain faith. Be assured that you are approaching a lighthouse on your journey where all will be illuminated and clarity restored. This could occur quite unexpectedly. There is an element of the sudden and the unexpected weaving into your reality at present.

It is likely that you have recently experienced endings and new beginnings and are now at the crossroads. You are unsure of the next step.

One phone call, one email or one chance encounter can change our lives in an instant. Be aware of new vibrant energy coming in around you and, in the meantime, count your blessings. Remember the saying, *When a fisherman can't go to sea, he stays home and mends his nets.* There is no point in stressing. Be assured that swift and positive change is imminent.

Lesson

Trust.

Power Choice

- Pray, meditate, read or draw.
- Spend time near the ocean.
- Remain alert for new opportunities.
- Believe in miracles.

Momentary Meditation

Imagine you are swimming in an ocean with a group of Mermaids and dolphins. You are happy, playful and carefree.

Affirmation

I am always divinely guided.

Liz's Comments

When I channelled this message, I sensed a magical element.

Many years ago, I had an uncanny experience involving an angel brooch that a dear friend had given to me. I wore it to a special event interstate and was devastated when I arrived home and realised it was gone. I searched my luggage and handbag but had no choice but to accept that the brooch was gone.

Two years later, I was home alone one morning, making coffee. Suddenly, I felt overshadowed by Spirit energy. In fact, it felt like there were many Spirits in the room.

I heard a voice inside my head clearly say, *Go to your handbag we have a present for you.* Feeling silly, I put my hand in my bag without looking and pulled out my lost angel brooch! This was physically impossible because the handbag I owned when I lost the brooch had been thrown out long ago. I gasped in disbelief and I heard the voice say. *We want you to remember that anything can happen and there are no limits.* Within moments the Spirit energy was gone and I was left staring at my brooch.

To this day, that brooch sits by my bedside to remind me daily that magic can definitely happen.

Believe that magic can happen for you too!

MESSAGE 10

·•⚹•·

Relationships

Messenger

Guardian Angel

Life is partly what we make it,
and partly what it is made by the friends we choose.
– Tennessee Williams

Vision

An angel pouring water from an urn as flowers instantly bloom.

Message

Your Guardian Angel is suggesting that it is time to review your relationships. Your Guardian Angel acts as your personal coach and cheerleader and simply encourages you to make choices that will serve your higher self.

Who uplifts you and who is looking out for you? Who makes you smile? Who makes you sad, feel inferior or lets you down? Is there someone you feel you have given more chances than they deserve? Rather than waste energy on holding grudges, use the power of choice wisely and surround yourself with those you trust knowing that they have your best interests at heart.

Weeding the garden of friendship and love will enable you to allow more love and positivity into your life, showering you with the love you seek and deserve.

Who we align ourselves with is so important. We are easily influenced by those around us and, as George Washington once said, *It is better to be alone than in bad company.*

Spirit is asking you to consider letting go of relationships that are not serving you. If they are meant to be in your life, they will come back to you shiny and new.

Lesson

Learning to create positive boundaries regarding relationships.

Power Choice

- Make an honest appraisal of your important relationships.
- Spend quality time with partners or those close to you.
- Communicate your deeper feelings.
- Bring roses into your home to bring positive energy regarding relationships.

Momentary Meditation

Visualise a vase full of different-coloured rose buds. Each rose represents a significant relationship in your life across all time and space. See each rose gently open and bloom. Sense and inhale the peace and harmony emanating from each bloom.

Affirmation

My relationships are always loving and uplifting.

Liz's Comments

This message is certainly wise but does not cover the complexities that relationships often present. What if the person who is affecting you negatively is your child, your mother, your best friend of fifty years or someone you are so attached to you don't want to let them go, regardless of the fallout.

Awareness is the first step. Considering the person in question and their effect on you is the beginning of an act of self-love.

Not all relationships need to end but sometimes they need to transform to a different level - which can be done! It may take time, boundary setting or clearer communication and definitely much love! Honesty, even if painful, can heal and uplift a wilting connection. If all else fails, sometimes we are left with no other choice but to create distance between ourselves and our loved ones.

Relationships are one of our biggest catalysts for growth and soul expansion as they challenge us to feel and dig deeply. They mirror depths of our souls we are not aware of.

An example in my life is the ever changing relationship I have had with my first husband who I first met in 1985.

In the beginning, we were friends for twelve months. We would set up blind dates for each other, have coffee, and hang out but initially there was no physical attraction.

Over time, something changed and we became girlfriend and boyfriend. This led to marriage. After seven years we became parents. Then we became divorced and became co-parents. Now that our child is a grown man, we are simply friends again.

Those chronological events don't include the deep varied feelings that ebbed and flowed through each stage of our relationship. It was at times soul destroying, uplifting, hurtful, loving, frustrating and certainly growth inducing. I am sure many of you have experienced this within your most karmic and important relationships.

The point is, if you cannot erase a person from your life that you feel is not in your best interest, see if you can shape-shift the relationship in a way that serves your higher self. If this seems impossible, it is time to hit the floor, pray from the heart and await divine guidance! Trust and be aware of synchronicities, strong feelings, and repetitive thoughts.

MESSAGE 11

• ·✳· •

Secrets

Messenger

Garden Fairy

A secret spoken finds wings.
– Robert Jordan

Vision

A Fairy with sheer golden wings places a finger to her lips.

Message

We all have secrets, some big and some small. Sometimes it's wise to keep secrets to ourselves and at other times it's wiser to share them.

Spirit wants you to know they are ready to listen and that you can unburden any secrets to them. You can communicate to your Spirit friends through talking, thinking or writing. Be authentic and know that they care.

Alternatively, there may be a special person in your life who will listen to you without judgement. If not, consider the vast availability of professional counselling and healing.

Maybe there is something you need to say to someone who you care about but it is of a confrontational nature and now it has become your secret. If this is the case, it is important that you express yourself or it may come out in a passive/aggressive manner which will not be helpful. Start by asking for help from the angels and Spirit. When you approach this person, come from your heart and lovingly express how you feel. You may want to begin by telling them how much you care for them.

If you have asked a specific question today, it may mean there is information regarding your question that you are not presently aware of.

The lower energies of guilt and shame are often associated with secrets. It is important you do not let these emotions saturate your soul as eventually they may manifest as ill health or imbalance.

Lesson

Accepting the shadow side of yourself.

Power Choice

- Express any guilt or shame.
- Share your secret with someone you trust.
- Consciously acknowledge self-forgiveness.
- Journal your secret.
- Research books or articles about people who held similar secrets.

Momentary Meditation

If possible, go outside and invite Fairy energy to help with this exercise.

Write down your secret and express your feelings. Hold the paper to your heart and say: *I now release any shame, guilt and burdensome emotions to the universe, I deserve understanding and unconditional love.*

Next, either carefully burn the paper or tear it up and throw it in the bin, with the intention of releasing. Know that your loving angels, guides, and the fairies were listening with unconditional love and without judgement.

Affirmation

I deserve to be heard.

Liz's Comments

My first memory of secrets was when I was a small child. I have recollections of adult whispers behind closed doors while I tried desperately to hear and understand what they were saying. It left me with a strange feeling in the pit of my stomach. My safe world was being intruded upon.

We live in a world that is too focused on what others may think and how we may be judged. This often results in people choosing not to seek support when they find themselves stuck in challenging situations. They are unsure how to navigate through them. A worst case scenario can even be suicide.

We all have secrets. How we deal with them is more important than having them.

As a young child I was embarrassed that I failed a test at school, particularly as the teacher clearly expressed her disappointment. I hid the result from my mother as I felt so ashamed. That shameful feeling stayed with me for years every time I recalled it. It wasn't the event so much as the feeling of being inadequate or not good enough. Perhaps if I had shared my feelings with someone, I could have processed them more positively by receiving reassurance from someone compassionate and understanding.

When we choose to *not* share a secret that is detrimental to us, we are not loving and caring for ourselves. If there is something you need to share that is burdening you, please seek support.

You can do so anonymously through online support or organisations such as Lifeline, here in Australia, that provides free telephone counselling. I also encourage you to journal your secret or attempt the momentary meditation above. Remember that you can always reach out to Spirit who is there to accept you with unconditional love.

MESSAGE 12

Transformation and Transition

Messenger

Butterfly

If you can't change your fate, change your attitude.
– Amy Tan

Vision

A colourful indigo Butterfly emerging from a cocoon.

Message

There is pain in being birthed and yet it is surely a miracle. There is an element of change weaving into your life at the moment. This may be subtle or it may be obvious.

The Spirit of the Butterfly wants you to know whatever burdens you feel you are carrying right now have a strong purpose and are part of the path you are meant to be walking. You have not lost your way.

These burdens are teaching you subtle lessons you may not currently understand and are somehow linked to your future path.

There may be days you have to dig deep within to find the strength you need but remember you are an important part of the universe. Some events and situations are chosen by our higher selves before we are born and we may not understand why until we return to our true home, the other side.

Often, in times of transformation and transition, there is an element of grief that will encompass our heart. Although grief is a difficult emotion to embrace, it transports us to the depths of our souls, creating seeds of pure wisdom. Rather than block the grief, it is healthier for our heart and soul to embrace it. Support is all around us if we seek it.

Lesson

Embracing fate, change, and transformation.

Power Choice

- It would be wise, at this time, to embrace internal and external challenges.
- Prepare for change.
- Seek support when needed.
- Be open to new ways of achieving results.
- Healing tools such as flower essences and Reiki can be helpful during times of change and transition.
- Remember that *gut* instincts are heightened during transitional times in life, listen to your hunches.

Momentary Meditation

Imagine you are watching a butterfly emerging from a cocoon, (alternatively, go online and watch a video so you can get the visual image). Shape-shift for a moment and feel like you are becoming the butterfly, free to move into the light. Focus on the joy and give thanks for the experience of transformation.

Affirmation

Change is a part of life and I am safe in the arms of the angels at all times.

Liz's Comments

This message speaks of change that is more fate-based, rather than choice-based. Forces are at work which may feel out of your control. This need not be negative change, just life's natural rhythm of degeneration and renewal.

Like many of you, I have experienced major transitions in life. Perhaps one of the most earth shattering changes for me was becoming a parent. I am always fascinated by new parents who seem so comfortable in their new role and take it all in their stride. I was not so graceful. I loved my first child immensely from the moment he was born, but it turned my world upside down.

My sleep and dietary patterns, my friends, my relationships, and my whole perception of life shifted, never to be the same again. I became extremely anxious and chose to attend counselling which helped me immensely.

This message is a reminder that changes and transition are a natural part of life. From the moment we are born, we never cease changing as each day we are allocated here on Earth will see us moving forward regardless of our resistance.

Change *is* challenging, yet challenges are what make us wiser and stronger.

Now is a perfect time to find some quality quiet time to reflect on the current shifts and changes and to ask for clear guidance from your loved ones in Spirit, your angels, and guides. Butterflies are also a personal sign for you at the moment, reassuring you that you are being guided and cared for and that everything will work out. Be aware of butterflies visiting you in a variety of guises including photographs or songs.

MESSAGE 13

— ·✳· —

Vulnerability

Messenger

Archangel Haniel

What makes you vulnerable, makes you beautiful.
– Brene Brown

Vision

An angel's hand places an umbrella of light over a sleeping child.

Message

The time has come to accept your vulnerability as an asset rather than a problem. Your sweet sensitivity acts as a conduit to higher forces, channelled guidance, and gifts of knowing.

Feeling sensitive allows us to get in touch with our true feelings so easily ignored in the fast-paced world we live in. Now is an opportunity to express your gratitude and love to someone special. You may feel inspired to perform a random act of kindness.

If specific circumstances have recently triggered your sense of vulnerability, be grateful that you have been reconnected with this precious part of yourself.

Now is not a time to *fix* things. It is a time to simply be in the present, acknowledging your inner child. Prayers for help and guidance are powerfully heard and responded to now. Be still, have faith.

The beauty in feeling sensitive is that our sense of joy can be enhanced. Engaging in activities that bring us joy and a light heart is recommended at this time.

If you have had any recent health problems, check that allergies are not involved as increased sensitivity can filter into our physical world.

If you have asked a specific question today, the answer may be to get in touch with your vulnerable side to access a new perspective.

Lesson

Accepting your vulnerability.

Power Choice

- Be diligent with spiritual protection.
- Pray, meditate, journal.
- Avoid harsh environments and those who distress you.
- Create a safe space.
- Be mindful of foods or beverages that are mood altering.
- Call on Archangel Haniel for assistance.
- Retreat into nature.

Momentary Meditation

Journey in your mind to a rose quartz crystal cave. Simply sit and absorb the loving energy. Pink rays of light bounce off the crystals. Bathe in the light.

Affirmation

I am at peace with all aspects of myself, I am safe.

Liz's Comments

There are times in life when one feels like lying in a foetal position on a couch under a blanket! There are other days where we feel we can conquer the world. Neither one is good nor bad, it is what it is. There is a part of our logical mind that likes to categorise our responses to life into good and bad. This is a message of reassurance that it is okay to accept your inner child and *any* feelings that are currently arising within you.

I suffered from anxiety attacks for many years. There were days I felt uncomfortable being in public in case people saw my vulnerability. I believed I was doing something wrong by feeling this way and it was not until I studied counselling that I began to work through my anxiety in my own way. It took time and acceptance of myself and was not always easy. Eventually I healed my condition and was able to accept myself more holistically and I now see the anxiety was a blessing in disguise.

Human experience is like a diamond, each facet offering insight and ultimately enhanced compassion for one another. We can choose to honour all aspects of ourselves, enhancing the joy that comes with living authentically.

MESSAGE 14

— ❖ —

Heart Healing

Messenger

The Fairy of the Pink Rose

It's not selfish to love yourself, take care of yourself
and to make your happiness your priority, it's necessary.
– Mandy Hale

Vision

A pink rose blooms, radiating sparkling white light, forming into
the shape of a fairy.

Message

Your heart is weary and has carried many burdens in your life, many
not your own. Your compassion and care for others is a wonderful
trait you possess but it is time to give your burdens to Spirit, so you
can create more room in your life for giving energy to what makes
your own heart sing.

We all prefer to avoid disappointing others at some point in our lives. It's an uncomfortable feeling letting others down. Life is about give and take, but there comes a time when our own happiness has to be a priority if we are to move forward and maximise our joy in life.

Disappointing others may be inevitable by making wise choices for yourself, and Spirit understands your hesitation. However, you are being asked to remember that by placing yourself first, you are ultimately serving your loved ones and all who come in contact with you.

Some of your close relationships may need reviewing or adjusting at this time and by opening to healing of your own heart, these relationships benefit.

Be at peace through living your life as your authentic self.

If you have asked a specific question today the answer lies in placing your needs as a priority.

Lesson

Valuing and responding to your true heart's desires.

Power Choice

- Seek counselling with a professional or close friend.
- Prioritise what your needs are.
- Be receptive to healing and receiving.
- Acknowledge and honour your deep desires.

Momentary Meditation

In a relaxed state, think of those you feel you may currently be disappointing by your choices. Imagine a cord of love from your heart to theirs. Send loving thoughts and feelings. Choose the higher road, choose self love.

Affirmation

I love and respect myself at all times.

Liz's Comments

This message is urging you to love yourself enough to choose what feels right for you, regardless of the reactions of others. The responses you fear may be unfounded. Assuming how someone will react may not serve you at this time. The reactions of others are not your problem. Spirit is urging you to follow your deep desires without fear or guilt.

Perhaps you have to let your boss or your lover down, or maybe even your children, so that your needs can be met.

When my first-born son was barely two years old, I was suffering from anxiety, feeling alone and isolated. I had recently divorced and was adjusting to being a single mother.

I had an opportunity to go on vacation for a week with some girlfriends but it was to a retreat where children weren't welcome. Every part of me felt it was just what I needed. I felt guilty leaving my son with a couple, who were also parents, as I had never been away from him before. However, I did go and it was exactly what I needed. The joy of coming home to my beautiful boy was euphoric. I came back refreshed and ready to take on the next challenges that life presented. My son was in good hands and was able to play with my friend's children while I was gone.

If we don't put our own needs first, we risk burning out or simply remaining unhappy. Choose you, be happy.

MESSAGE 15

·※·

Peace Pipe

Messenger

Native American Elder

Imagine all the people, living life in peace.
– John Lennon

Vision

The Messenger adorned with eagle feathers raises his arms, holding
a peace pipe.

Message

The gentle energy of the peace pipe appears on your path today. It is
a reminder that a loving and tender approach to yourself and others
will bring multiple blessings.

Where there has been conflict among groups, individuals, or within
oneself, the peace pipe signifies that drama is ending and peace can

now begin. You are asked to remember that holding on to bitter or sad thoughts can be toxic to your body, mind, and soul.

All relationships reflect our inner world and we can learn much about ourselves by owning what we see in other people. Each relationship in our life is a teacher for us on some level.

We are all part of each other as the universal life-force links us together as one. Bless all the meaningful connections in your life. Each one has helped shape who you are and bestowed wisdom in your soul. Significant people are like earth angels – embrace and honour their presence in your life.

You are supported more than you know by those living and in the Spirit world.

If you have asked a specific question, the answer lies in either finding peace in a relationship or seeking advice from someone you trust, so they can reflect what you need to see in yourself at this time.

Lesson

Surrendering conflict, choosing the higher path.

Power Choice

- Forgive yourself and others.
- Accept that we all have a light and a shadow within.
- Focus on the good in yourself and others.
- Create a list of everyone you have had meaningful connections with and mentally send your gratitude and

blessings to each one. Include any group associations such as classmates, work colleagues, hospitals and so on.

Momentary Meditation

Imagine you are sitting with a Tribal Elder beside a brilliant fire in a forest. It is a perfectly still evening and the moon is full. You focus on the embers rising from the fire. As each ember rises you feel less burdened and more relaxed. Absorb the calm presence of the elder beside you. You now manifest peace in all your relationships.

Affirmation

Peace permeates all my relationships.

Liz's Comments

My favourite part of this message was the words: *Each relationship in our life is a teacher for us on some level.* This relates even to those who irritate us. It is said that what we find difficult to accept in others, mirrors an aspect of ourselves, which can be quite confronting.

Perhaps these people are sent to us to aid our self-development and healing. Acceptance of self and others, including flaws, is the mark of a mature and wise soul.

I had a strict teacher in primary school who terrified me with her stern looks and regular punishment. It was the 1960s and striking children with a cane was legal. She caned the boys and occasionally rapped a large ruler over the girls' hands. It was usually for something minor, like talking in class or not paying attention.

Despite her punishments, this teacher also taught thoroughly how to write and speak correctly, offered challenging maths puzzles, and encouraged intelligent debating and problem solving. She certainly had a strong influence on my young mind.

Although it was a difficult class for a sensitive child such as myself to be part of, I learned resilience, strength, and that I was smarter than I realised. Interestingly, I did not relate to any of the other children in that class which, in retrospect, supported my evolving independence.

It is no accident that an influential person or group is in your life at the moment. The first person or group that comes to mind is likely to be the connection Spirit is helping you with. Find the gift in each connection, be at peace, and move on if it is in your best interest. Otherwise, accept them for who they are which will help you to accept yourself, warts and all.

MESSAGE 16

—•⋇•—

Protection

Messenger

Violet Water Lily Fairies

We are all fairies, living underneath a leaf of a lily pad.
– Tori Amos

Vision

Violet-coloured water lilies dance upon a still lake.

Message

The Water Fairies bring you blessings of spiritual cleansing and protection. Just as we need to cleanse our physical bodies regularly, our spiritual bodies also need clearing and protecting.

It is possible that you have unknowingly taken on someone else's emotions and are now feeling as if they are your own. If you are feeling sadness or discomfort, ask yourself – *Are these my feelings?*

Have I been around a person who is struggling or possibly in an environment that was unpleasant?

As we evolve we become more sensitive to energy. It is likely that, as you have this book in your hands, you are a light worker or a sensitive soul. The Water Fairies are here to remind you and assist you in clearing your energy and sealing it with their protective violet lilies. There is great benefit in weaving spiritual cleansing and protection methods into your daily routine.

If there is a specific issue you have asked about today, the message is to clear your energy and then ask yourself if you have more clarity. It would also be wise to clear the energy of this book as perhaps another's energy has infiltrated it. (Instructions on page XXXV.)

Experiment with some of the spiritual protection methods listed below under Power Choice.

Lesson

Becoming aware of subtle energy within and around you.

Power Choice

- Ask Spirit and the fairies for spiritual protection daily.
- See an egg-shaped sphere of white or purple light around yourself regularly with the intention of creating spiritual protection.
- Ask the Water Fairies for assistance.
- See cords of negativity being cut between yourself and others. You can call on Archangel Michael and his divine sword of protection to assist you with this process.

- Use an amethyst crystal as a protection tool.
- Enjoy a lavender and salt bath or swim in the ocean.
- Burn sage, or use an essential oil such as lavender to clear your energy field and your environment.

Momentary Meditation

Imagine you are lying on a floating bed in the centre of a still lake. Tiny, healing Water Fairies are giving you a magical healing. They place violet water lilies all around you. Breathe deeply; accept the healing and protection they bestow upon you.

Affirmation

I am divinely protected at all times.

Liz's Comments

Recently I had an encounter with a client who was experiencing a great deal of grief. Nothing unusual in my line of work, except that this particular day I had had a small family crisis at home before she arrived, and in the rush I had forgotten to spiritually protect myself before the reading. It didn't seem to affect the reading and all went well.

Two hours later I found myself sobbing in the bathroom. Nothing had happened. My family crisis was resolved and there was absolutely nothing to be sad about and yet I felt like I had lost my best friend. Amongst my sobs, I heard my guide's voice in the distance say, *stop and think about it.* It caught me by surprise and I stopped sobbing.

I clearly saw my client's face in my mind's eye and felt her pain and sadness. Of course, it was so obvious, I had overlooked it. I then knew what to do. I had a salt and lavender bath which is wonderful for cleansing unwanted energy. I sent distance healing to the client, mentally closed all my chakra centres and visualised a shield of white light around myself. The grief and sadness I was feeling instantly dissipated.

It is easy to take on another's energy in your workplace, in a family environment, and sometimes even in a public place such as a train or supermarket. The more sensitive you are, the more important it is to learn what protective methods work for you and apply them regularly.

MESSAGE 17

・❈・

Empty Vessel

Messenger

Japanese Zen Master

Empty your cup so that it may be filled:
become devoid to gain totality.
– Bruce Lee

Vision

Empty floral-painted tea cups.

Message

You may be feeling numb or empty within or perhaps it is time to release any negative or toxic energy. When it feels as though life has worn us down, a sense of surrender emerges which takes us deeper into our authentic selves. Be assured, regardless of how you may be feeling, that this can be a beneficial time.

The beauty of feeling like an empty vessel is that you can then receive exactly what you need, even if it is not what you want. Now is a time of fine-tuning your inner world so that your external world will benefit.

Part of you has let go of outcomes, a truly fortunate place to be. Trust is now the light that illuminates the path ahead and you are in a position to feel more peace and a deeper connection to your higher self and the universe.

If you have asked a specific question, the answer lies in giving your concern to a higher power and letting go of outcomes.

Remember that everything does happen for a reason. Prepare to receive without expectation.

Lesson

Strengthening faith in self and cosmic forces.

Power Choices

- Declutter your environment and inner world.
- Consciously name what no longer serves you.
- Review your diet.
- Book a health or spiritual retreat.
- Detox your body.

Momentary Meditation

Sitting quietly, think about what no longer serves you in your life. Imagine you are standing beside a still lake. You pick up a stone to throw into the lake and as you throw it you have the intention of releasing one thing that no longer serves you. Continue to throw as many stones as you desire. Breathe deeply, and give thanks.

Affirmation

I am ready to receive; all my needs are met.

Liz's Comments

When we have given all we can give, or seemingly done all we can do, we understand the meaning of letting go. This message is a reassurance that this state of being is actually a progressive place to be.

Whatever concerns you right now, this message is advising you to not overthink things, to surrender, and relax. More will be revealed shortly and relief is in sight. Change is inevitable. Silent time with yourself and the universe is the best way forward at the moment.

At the end of an intense relationship I had many years ago, I wandered around for days feeling numb with disappointment. After a month passed, I caught myself in the mirror and saw the sadness in my eyes. Something inside me flared up with anger which fuelled me to shift something. I cleaned my house from top to bottom and removed any items that reminded me of the relationship. I bought a shovel and dug up the vegetable garden. I went to a sacred place in nature and did a releasing ritual. I felt like I was coming back into my body again and began to feel like my old self.

We all give our power away at some time in our lives to people, places or things and it is a valuable lesson to take it back.

Whatever it is that you need to *empty* at the moment, know that it is a natural part of a cycle in life where you can create an even larger cup to receive.

MESSAGE 18

—•☀•—

Manifesting

Messenger

Mountain Spirit

The most valuable skill or talent that you could ever develop
is that of directing your thoughts to what you want.
– Abraham-Hicks

Vision

A glorious mountain covered with wild blooms in the springtime, a
face embedded in the mountain.

Message

This is a message of reassurance that the energy and hard work you
have been giving out will soon be rewarded. The light at the end of
the tunnel may yet be elusive, but only temporarily.

The Spirit of the Mountain energy is solid and supportive and reassures
you that you have wonderful powers of manifestation. Clarity of

thought marrying practical action is the key and soon your needs will be met in solid and practical ways. Keep striving for improvement in areas of life that are meaningful to you. Create practical structures in your life that support you, your lifestyle and your loved ones.

The flowers blooming on the mountain in the springtime represent positive outcomes and reaping rewards. The seeds you have sown in the past, and continue to sow, will blossom and grow.

Keep doing whatever you are doing. Trust there is a bigger plan at work that may manifest in an even better way than you previously thought. Dismiss any fears and doubts troubling you, own your power and keep moving forward.

If you have asked a specific question today, the answer is to have faith in yourself and know your needs are about to be met.

Whether you are conscious of it or not, you are currently creating strong foundations for the future which will have a positive ripple effect on others.

Lesson

Your soul is experimenting with outcomes of actions.

Power Choice

- Use manifestation techniques to boost desired outcomes.
- Create a vision board.
- Breathe your desired reality into the now.
- Use positive affirmations.
- Study mentors or employ a life coach.

Momentary Meditation

Imagine you are on a beach at sunrise, visualise what you want to manifest in the sky above. See it, feel it, sense it, and say the words, *It is done, it is so.*

Affirmation

I create a joyful and meaningful life every day.

Liz's Comments

It is said that everything happens for a reason and, to some extent, I believe that is true. Yet hard work and effort do bring rewards and we have more power to manifest than we realise. We are only scratching the surface of our own infinite, innate power.

When we feel inspired to take action, it is often Spirit guiding us. It seems we are on an ongoing journey learning to listen to the subtle voices of our soul. We co-create our life with the universe much like an artist's paintbrush brings life to a canvas.

This message is acknowledging the hard work you have been doing and praises you for your efforts. There is more to reap that you may not yet be aware of.

When my husband and I were awaiting approval for a home loan to buy our house, we were on edge. We had done all the right things, worked hard, saved the money for the deposit and employed a broker. I had created an altar with a green candle for abundance and a photo of the house we wanted to buy. I would stop and say prayers at the altar regularly hoping this would help to manifest our desired outcome.

Finally, we received a response from the broker. The bank agreed to grant the loan on the condition that we came up with another $10,000! There was no way we could find that sort of money and our hearts sank. We had tried so hard.

The next day I met with an old friend and shared what had happened. Unknown to me, my friend had recently come into some money and she offered to help us. It was so random and unexpected!

It felt as though universal synchronicity was at work and we accepted her kind offer and the house was ours. Obviously I was also blessed to have such a kind-hearted friend.

My point is, the saying, *God helps those who help themselves*, is quite true.

Whatever is happening in your life, wherever you have been giving of yourself and your energy, you are about to reap the rewards, so rejoice!

MESSAGE 19

Patience

Messenger

A Prophet of the Dawn

There will be an answer, let it be.
– Paul McCartney

Vision

A pale blue robe adorns a male figure; his arms open to receive the morning light.

Message

This message is to alert you that by practising patience, you allow yourself time to reassess your current direction. The way forward is to take time out, reach out for support, and attempt to gain an objective view of your present reality.

Spirit understands it can be difficult to gain objectivity when we are attached to outcomes and this is part of the complexity of being human.

Coming from a place of logic is helpful but only when it is balanced and in alignment with your gut instincts. This requires you to make a conscious effort to slow down and listen to the subtle whispers of your soul. When a sense of peace envelops you, things will naturally move forward.

Whatever you now face, know that you are supported by invisible forces in Spirit, including the Prophet of the Dawn. Resolutions will be enhanced by taking a quiet and surrendered approach.

Remain optimistic, the vision implies that by being patient the sun will rise in perfect timing – you only need to be open to its arrival. Greet the dawn with positive anticipation.

Lesson

Living authentically and taking time to listen to your inner guidance.

Power Choice

- Take time out for reflection and prayer to access the answers you seek.
- Visualise the Prophet of the Dawn in your mediations and ask for further guidance.
- Sit with your feelings, even if it is for a short time. Breathe through them.
- In still moments, ask for guidance from the heart.
- Use nature as your meditation vessel.

Momentary Meditation

Visualise yourself on a high mountain, a glorious view below. The Prophet of the Dawn sits beside you. See the issues that concern you unfolding below, allowing an objective viewpoint to emerge. Notice what insights come as you observe.

Affirmation

I trust the process of life.

Liz's Comments

Often, when I draw the *Patience* card in an angel or tarot deck, my shoulders drop and I let out a loud sigh. Who wants to be patient when we have pressing situations that need action now? When situations are getting us down, it's natural to want to work through things as quickly as possible.

As I grow older, patience has become my friend. I now believe that there is wisdom in the saying, *Good things come to those who wait.*

Patience can be likened to a sculptor's tool, gently smoothing the harsh edges of our inner restlessness. Patience creates time to brainstorm options, consider alternatives, and question what we want, including how to obtain it. Patience gives us space to heal and work with divine timing, allowing the universe to reveal it's well-laid plans.

There is an element of surrender when we are forced to wait. Let it be.

MESSAGE 20

·❉·

Body Wisdom

Messenger

Earth Fairies

The eyes are the window to your soul.
– William Shakespeare

Vision

Transparent fairies radiate divine light as they chop wood and gather flowers.

Message

Our bodies are intrinsically linked to our heart and our soul and have more power than we are aware of.

The fae of the Earth are here to ground you into your body so you can sense and feel its wisdom. Your body is an oracle of guidance and divination. If you are still enough within yourself, you can access and decipher its messages.

For example, when we don't express our truth, we may experience throat issues; when we hear words that are unpleasant, our ears may suffer or, when we worry about the future, we may have vision problems.

If you have recently experienced any physical dis-ease or imbalance, consider the emotional causes and meaning for insight and questioning. You may be enlightened by the answers you find.

Our bodies also respond in synch with our innate intuition. We know when something doesn't feel right, usually in our stomach. Our hair stands on end when we feel danger. Your body has a message for you – listen, and trust your gift of intuition.

If you have asked a specific question today, experiment with the meditation below to help you access the answers you seek.

Lesson

Aligning your physical self with your emotional and spiritual bodies.

Power Choices

- Call on the healing fairies, healing angels and guides.
- Be kind to your body and honour it in a way that works for you.
- Look up Louise Hay's meanings for physical imbalances in her book *Love Your Body*.

- Meditate on the areas of your body that need attention and ask the question, *How can I serve you?*
- Ask the fae to direct you to the perfect healer.
- Practice yoga, walk often, and breathe deeply.
- Nourish yourself with high energy foods.
- Make an appointment for a chakra balance.
- Ground yourself by hugging trees, going barefoot, playing a drum or doing a grounding meditation.

Lesson

Balancing the body with the heart and soul.

Momentary Meditation

Breathe deeply and ponder on a question with which you need guidance. Consider a course of action – how does your body respond? Does it feel relaxed or tense? Practise using your body's responses as a guidance tool and you may be pleasantly surprised with the results.

Affirmation

My body is an oracle of wisdom.

Liz's Comments

When I look back on my life, I am amazed at how much my body and I have been through and I am sure most people feel the same. From the moment we are born our bodies are working for us twenty-four hours a day, performing a zillion functions and processes each moment.

I often talk to my body in the third person. I asked it recently if it would like to go to a yoga class and I felt all the cells jumping with joy saying, *Yes!* Perhaps I am eccentric, but I find this approach helps me to be more in tune with my body's needs.

I notice during times of major change in my life that my body often becomes ill or imbalanced. I feel this happens when I resist the flow of life and feel a lack of control. I have friends who have said that this is true for them also. Flexibility can be a blessing for our bodies and selves in times of change.

My first child was born blue with no life in him and we all held our breath while the doctors worked on him. After several minutes, the sound of his cry was music to everyone present. I have often wondered if his soul was standing beside that tiny body trying to decide whether he really wanted to be here.

It is our soul that brings life to our bodies and it is our soul that leaves behind an empty shell when we pass away. Our bodies, minds, and souls are a team that prefers to work in harmony. The body is a gift that continues to baffle medical research. The message here today is to honour your body and be open to hearing the messages it brings.

MESSAGE 21

•—✷—•

Celebration

Messenger

Archangel Mariel

The more you praise and celebrate your life,
the more there is in life to celebrate.
– Oprah Winfrey

Vision

Pink and purple flower petals falling from a turquoise-coloured sky.

Message

The energy of great joy is approaching you. Something you have been longing for can now materialise easily and naturally. There is no need to push or force issues or situations. Everything is working out exactly as it should.

Being open and receptive to joy is your challenge now. Allow past disappointments to dissipate as you safely release protective barriers that are no longer useful. Spirit understands your predicament and is eager to see you happy and uplifted. You deserve the best possible outcomes.

Archangel Mariel is asking you to trust your higher wisdom and embrace opportunities as they now present themselves.

If you have asked a specific question today, you are assured a happy outcome and are advised to project only positive thoughts around this situation. You may be hearing of celebrations such as weddings, birthdays or conceptions.

You may find there will be three opportunities in a short amount of time, be observant and ready. It is safe to be your authentic self. It is time to be open to the magic of possibilities outside of your usual comfort zone.

Lesson

Learning to recognise and embrace joy.

Power Choices

- Avoid self-sabotage behaviours or patterns from the past.
- Be your own best friend and make choices that serve yourself.
- Consider all opportunities that are presented to you.
- Accept invitations to celebrations.

Momentary Meditation

See yourself standing outside in a beautiful place in nature with your arms wide open. You look to the sky and see pink and purple petals gently falling. Each petal that touches you brings a feeling of joy, you are blessed.

Affirmation

I now fully accept joy and abundance into my life.

Liz's Comments

I believe one of the secrets of receiving joy is feeling worthy enough to accept it. When you think about it, joy is everywhere, from the birds singing in the trees to a child's laughter in the street. Whatever we focus on immediately elicits various thoughts and emotions. When we focus on joy, we feel uplifted.

Another secret to receiving joy is being consciously grateful for the joy that already exists in our lives and in simple moments. When we use descriptive words and include how something makes us feel in our gratitude thoughts or writings, the vibration of gratitude is enhanced. The power of a gratitude journal cannot be underestimated.

For example, we can say, *I am grateful for my son* or we can say *I am grateful for my beautiful, cheeky, vibrant son who makes me feel there is an abundance of unconditional love in my life.* The latter sentence sends out a loud echo to the universe and you will receive blessings back tenfold.

When my dog Charlie has his beloved ball, he is in total joy. He is so in the moment and everything else ceases to exist. His joy spreads and before I know it I am smiling and laughing.

This message is asking you to be alert to opportunities of joy coming in around you and to know that you are certainly worthy of receiving them.

Every drop of joy expands and touches others. Allow joy into your life.

MESSAGE 22

---·※·---

Digging Deep

Messenger

An English Maiden

When all doors are shut and you have nowhere to go,
that is when you go within. Every crisis is an
opportunity and you are the beginning.
– Sri Sri Ravi Shankar

Vision

An English maiden, dressed in blue velvet, fetches water from a
deep well.

Message

Beneath the surface, there is an untold story that only you have the
key to unlock.

Spirit is encouraging you to go deep within while setting the
intention to get to the root cause of the issue you are inquiring

about. If you have chosen this message as a general reading there may be something you are not acknowledging that prevents you from experiencing optimum joy in your life.

A piece of a jigsaw is presently missing in the bigger scheme of things and, by addressing a deeper issue, epiphanies and realisations will put everything into perspective.

Exploring unfinished business from childhood, past or present relationships, and past-life issues may be relevant now.

If you have asked a specific question, the answer is that clearing inner blocks will reset the flow around your query.

Spirit will support you as you go within and search for deeper meaning. Remember, there is an abundance of resources, tools and support at your fingertips.

Lesson

Going within, knowing yourself on a deeper level.

Power Choices

- Look for classes/courses that guide you to go within.
- Seek out a psychologist or past-life therapist who resonates with you.
- Honour your needs, schedule some *me time*.
- Go on a vision quest, spend time in nature or at a health retreat.
- Schedule a clairvoyant reading or spiritual healing.
- Ask for guidance in your dream state.

Momentary Meditation

In a relaxed state, imagine you are sitting in a green field surrounded by a circle of sacred stones. The stones emanate a light and a frequency that are helping you to unlock the answers you seek within. You ask yourself the question *'What do I need to know right now that will help me move forward?'* Take the first thought or feeling that comes. Be aware of relative signs in the next few days.

Affirmation

I find peace with my inner world.

Liz's Comments

I have had some amazing experiences when researching my deeper, inner realms. In the 1980's I experimented with rebirthing, which was popular at the time. I relived my physical birth in my current lifetime and released some beliefs I had brought in with me. I have experienced past-life regressions and seen myself in various scenarios, often with themes that were relatable to whatever challenges I faced at the time.

I believe there is an element of fear, for many of us, of going too deep in case we find something we won't know how to deal with. When we do feel the fear and do it anyway, a sense of empowerment embraces us.

It is easy to become *stuck* in our lives which may prevent us from living life to the fullest. An honest self-appraisal of our authentic feelings can uncover solutions to allow us to move forward and free ourselves up.

This message is reassuring that you will not uncover anything you cannot handle and encourages you to seek out practical support to guide you. Your prayers will be heard and the universe is happy to support you.

MESSAGE 23

Ritual and Ceremony

Messenger

Native American Shaman

We do not go into ceremony to talk about God,
we go into ceremony to talk with God.
– Quanah Parker, Comanche leader

Vision

Drums beat as a Shaman throws herbs on a fire and stars illuminate a night sky.

Message

Through the act of performing rituals and ceremonies, we formalise our communication with Spirit and pay tribute to our growth as a soul.

Celebrating new understandings on your journey here on Earth is a wonderful way to express gratitude, and honour your personal path.

Bless the mistakes you have made as they have made you who you are and impressed hard-earned wisdom onto your soul.

Ritual is a powerful way of setting intention, offering thanks to Great Spirit and shifting stubborn energy. Whether it is a ritual as simple as lighting a candle and saying a prayer, or doing something more elaborate, there is a window now where Spirit is requesting an audience with you. Expressing your true self to Spirit is an honour and you will be filled with a new influx of refreshing and loving energy.

If you have asked a specific question today, this message sincerely suggests you give the burden around this question to Spirit. This is the basis of ritual, making a conscious connection to Spirit through action and employing a higher power to assist you.

This message may also mean the energy of ritual is coming in around you, such as a wedding, a christening or a memorial.

Whether you need assistance with healing your heart or soul, manifesting, or simply honouring Spirit and giving thanks, now is the time to express to Great Spirit.

Lesson

Learning to communicate with Spirit in a practical way.

Power Choices

- Write a letter to Spirit so you can see what is in your heart.
- Set up a sacred space, such as an altar or a garden area, where you can sit and meditate – be creative.

- Research shamanism, ceremonies and vision quests.
- Consider doing your own ritual or with a group of trusted friends.
- Find a shamanic healer for healing, advice or training.

Momentary Meditation

Begin by sitting in front of either a real or imaginary candle. With a clear intention, light the candle. Ask Spirit from your heart whatever you would like help with, or what you would like to formally acknowledge. Once done, extinguish the candle while giving thanks. Trust that you have been heard.

Affirmation

Great Spirit hears me at all times and I honour our connection.

Liz's Comments

Indigenous nations have been aware of the power of rituals for eons and we can learn from their traditions. Most of us have had some experience of ritual such as attending a wedding or a religious occasion. There is a sense of unity at such occasions and some of us can also sense a subtle presence of Spirit.

In my personal experience, I have found an elevated vibration can be felt when participating in a ritual whether it is performed alone or in a group.

Recently I performed an informal ceremony with some of my students with the intention of creating more abundance in our lives.

The presence of Spirit's love and power seemed enhanced in the room and was felt by all who attended. It didn't seem to matter that we were in a Community Hall, rather than nature, as the power was coming from our sincere hearts, connecting to the unconditional love that was present.

We created an altar with candles, crystals, and flowers. Everyone placed handwritten prayers on the altar or kept their prayers privately in their heart. We acknowledged the Spirits of water, air, fire and earth as we played peaceful music and went within. As the ceremony progressed, the energy in the room was electric.

Within a few months we were all able to report a sense of new abundance had entered our lives in different ways, but perfectly tailored to each individual.

I have performed solo ceremonies at home, by the ocean, and in nature to release outdated patterns and relationships and to invoke healing. There are no limits or strict guidelines how to perform a ritual and I encourage you to be creative. If your intentions are sincere, I guarantee you will not be disappointed.

MESSAGE 24

Let Down Your Guard

Messenger

Hawaiian Dancer

You have to push through every barrier to get to the mountain top.
– Lailah Gifty Akita

Vision

A young Hawaiian girl dancing on golden sands, at sunset.

Message

Embrace love! Whether it comes from a loved one, or a new person entering your life, the time to open to love is now.

The peace you seek will not be found by hiding your true self. At some point, you made a subconscious or conscious decision to alienate yourself from the flow of life in some way. Your weary soul decided to retreat for its own self-preservation.

Perhaps you fear the intimacy of close friendships or love on a level you have not yet considered. Spirit understands your vulnerability but also wants to alert you to the fact that wonderful opportunities to receive love are either right in front of you or about to manifest. Spirit wants the best for you and urges you to be ready to accept love. Forgive yourself and the past and move on. A period of healing and reflection is ending.

If you asked a specific question today, the answer is to be alert and receptive to loving opportunities coming in around you, which will allay your current concern. Opportunities may appear in the form of new people entering your life or as an obvious sign.

Step into the light, release the past, new love awaits.

Lesson

Releasing outdated emotional patterns in order to receive the new.

Power Choice

- Seek counselling from a professional or a close friend.
- Choose to *reframe* the past.
- Declutter your environment in preparation for the new.
- Write a list describing what qualities you would like in a new partner.
- Consider flower essences as a healing tool at this time.

Momentary Meditation

Begin by consciously relaxing. Place one hand on your heart. Breathe in and out, gently focusing on the centre of your chest. Feel warmth flooding your chest and imagine cobwebs in your heart dissolving to white light. Envisage the white light encircling your chest. Recite the affirmation below. There is now more room in your heart centre to accept more love into your life.

Affirmation

I am open to receiving an abundance of pure love and support.

Liz's Comments

When I had the vision of a Hawaiian girl dancing on the beach, I was filled with a wonderful feeling of inner freedom and abandonment. I sense that Spirit's desire for you is to live life to the fullest where areas of love are concerned. Too much of our precious time here on Earth is wasted and opportunities missed through our limited thinking. It is time to think outside the square and creatively assess other ways of looking at situations.

Visiting the beach at sunset recently, I was astonished that no other person was present, as I live in a tourist area. Although it is not a busy beach, it was unusual for it to be deserted. A light ignited inside me and I grabbed the opportunity. I ran along the shoreline with my hands in the air yelling at the top of my voice, *Thank you!* It was wonderful to experience the feeling of complete abandonment while taking in the glory of the ocean setting. I felt like a child again. I went home uplifted and refreshed. My run on the beach reflects the feeling that came with this message.

Whatever you are faced with now, being open to love in all its wondrous forms is the answer.

MESSAGE 25

——•❉•——

Set Your Own Standards

Messenger

Archangel Gabriel

Define success on your own terms, achieve by your own rules
and build a life you are proud to live.
— Anne Sweeney

Vision

An angel holding a burning torch, lighting up the night sky and
revealing unseen shadows.

Message

This is a time of epiphanies. You can now see that it is acceptable
to be exactly who you are and do things in your own unique way.
Comparing yourself to others and putting unrealistic expectations
upon yourself can literally become a thing of the past.

Getting in touch with your inner courage and deeper guidance is a winning combination, not necessarily in a worldly sense, but in expressing your own authenticity. Where you have held back for fear of not being understood or accepted, are clues to where you can now break through.

Stand joyous in your truth and people will respond with respect and admiration. If you have been holding back the truth from someone you care about, now is the time to reveal your true feelings and thoughts.

If you have asked a specific question today, the answer is to hold the space of authenticity and move forward from there. You do not need to fit into another's ideas of who you are. You cannot fail if you are true to yourself and others.

Lesson

Honouring your own uniqueness.

Power Choices

- Allow yourself to be creative in thought and action.
- Write or speak your truth with love.
- Tell others your true feelings.
- Do mirror work; look into your own eyes and say positive affirmations.
- Allow encouraging people to surround you.

Momentary Meditation

Imagine you are sitting by a still lake on a perfect day. You see your reflection in the water which reveals your inner beauty. Say the affirmation below.

Affirmation

I honour my unique self; it is safe to be me.

Liz's Comments

When I was writing my first book, *For the Love of Spirit, A Medium Memoir*, I was concerned others would judge me when I revealed personal aspects of myself. My self-doubt and lack of confidence surfaced often.

I had a vivid dream that I was talking to, whom I refer to as a prophet of peace, John Lennon. I have always been a big fan of John, so whether I projected his energy into the dream, or perhaps I met him in the spirit world, I am not sure. We talked of many things but the one thing he said, in his English accent, that stayed with me when I awoke was, *You don't have to play by the rules, make up your own rules.*

After this wonderful dream, I was filled with a new surge of energy when writing the book and felt reassured it was okay to express my unique take on things. This is what beauty, art, people, and life are all about – uniqueness. We can choose to be proud of our differences rather than believe we have to hide them.

This message urges you to reveal yourself. Strip away the layers of illusion based on fear and approval seeking. Be brave, be you!

MESSAGE 26

• ❈ •

Warming

Messenger

Bear

We choose to forget aspects of ourselves and
then we forget that we've forgotten.
– Debbie Ford

Vision

A large brown bear grunts loudly as he stands proudly on a mountain top.

Message

Bears often appear as a symbol of healing. Healing occurs when we experience balance and harmony with all aspects of ourselves.

When we neglect certain parts of ourselves, they become cold and stagnant. Where our focus goes, activation occurs. The healing energy of the Bear longs to flood warmth into the areas that have been become cold.

Do not fear reactivating a dormant area of yourself, particularly if the reason it became dormant was due to heartache. If we were hurt in a past relationship, we may shut down to the possibilities of new opportunities to love. We risk missing out on something wonderful.

Part of the healing element of this message is to prompt you to redirect your focus to areas of your life that you actually love. Perhaps they have been forgotten or you have had little time to devote to them.

What is it that warms your heart? What gives you joy? The answers you are seeking at the moment will come to you more easily when you are feeling joy and are in your element.

If you have asked a specific question today, the answer lies in activating a forgotten part of yourself that brings you joy and then clarity will be yours.

Lesson

Reactivating forgotten gems within yourself.

Power Choice

- Re-prioritise your time schedule.
- Create a list of life areas that have become *cold*.
- Seek inspiration through mentors or creative work.
- Call on the Spirit of the Bear for healing and guidance.
- Recall something you enjoyed doing in the past and consider reactivating this activity into your life.

Momentary Meditation

Sitting quietly, reactivate hidden joy by recalling one happy memory as a child. It may have been a simple moment such as climbing a tree, hearing a story or hugging someone. Focus on how the event made you feel. Absorb and allow feelings of joy to flood your being.

Affirmation

I feel joyfully alive and complete.

Liz's Comments

I enjoyed the vision that accompanied this message. The large Brown Bear appeared with such force, intuiting a wonderful electric shot of healing energy. It felt like being woken from a deep sleep.

Recently as I walked through the country side, I spontaneously had a flashback to being sixteen years old. I think the memory was triggered by a scent in the air and for a few moments I felt young, free, and in wonder of nature. I had that sense that anything was possible.

Our souls are made of an indestructible force that cannot be tainted, regardless of what we encounter and how we deal with life. I sense this message is asking us to connect with that force that never really dies, even if it has been quiet lately. We all unintentionally direct our energy into people, places, and things that do not always serve us.

Reassess what is important to you and place yourself first to achieve balance. From a point of balance and clarity, forward movement flows.

MESSAGE 27

·✳·

Magic

Messenger

Raven

The world is full of magic things, patiently waiting for
our senses to grow sharper.
– W.B. Yeats

Vision

A raven sitting on a branch, poised, its gaze to the sky.

Messenger

There is magic brewing under the surface of your life in some regard.
A series of synchronistic events will soon unfold which will reveal
a plan orchestrated by divine planning. On a subtle level, you can
sense this shift approaching. Do not dismiss your deeper knowing.

This is a time to celebrate by communing with Spirit and listening
to the whispers of your soul. Quiet your mind and give thanks in

advance for the magic and beauty of living and breathing. Listen to the magic in the silence.

Raven now advises you to prepare to witness miracles and magic. Be open to the unusual and things outside your normal range of experience. The series of events which are about to unfold will be a surprise to you but will provide exactly what you need now.

There is no need to change your daily routine but rather prepare yourself energetically for the magic you are about to experience. Attempt to be in receptive mode and release doubts that do not serve you.

If you have asked a specific question the answer may not be available immediately but will reveal itself shortly in a way that is an obvious sign from Spirit. If you have a major decision to make, the message is to stall for a short time. Soon, everything will be crystal clear.

Magic is afoot!

Lesson

Accepting the divinity of life and Spirit.

Power Choice

- Prepare by meditating.
- Seek emotional healing.
- Do not assume you know the bigger picture, have faith.
- Clear your path and await the magic.
- Ask for signs from Spirit.
- Be aware of black feathers on your path or sightings of black birds.

Momentary Meditation

Imagine a flock of Ravens circling the sky, their black wings moving in unison. A rainbow appears and the birds shape-shift into golden beams of light as they merge into the rainbow. Breathe in the rainbow light a few times - the magic is now with and within you.

Affirmation

Magic happens.

Liz's Comments

Birds are messengers of Spirit and they have the uncanny knack of turning up in our lives at auspicious moments. I am sure many of you reading this have experienced a special bird moment.

When I visited Hawaii, I was in awe of the pink flamingos living in a pond in the lobby of the motel where I stayed. Their elegant grace and beauty was uplifting. On another occasion, when an owl swooped in front of my windscreen while driving home one dark night, my whole being was delighted as the encounter felt so personal.

When I see magpie birds I think of my deceased father and if they turn up at an auspicious moment I know it is his way of saying *Hello* and that he has my back.

Magic does exist, whether we are conscious of it or not. I sense this message is to remind you that we can choose to not only acknowledge magic, but also to prepare, as there is definitely a wave of magic coming in around you.

MESSAGE 28

Romance

Messenger

Goddess Guinevere

To love oneself is the beginning of a lifelong romance.
– Oscar Wilde

Vision

Guinevere stands in a field of red roses and opens her arms to receive.

Message

Focusing on the beauty within and around us creates a vibration of romance. Becoming aware of raindrops on a window pane, the colourful wings of a butterfly or the taste of honey as it touches your tongue, are all forms of romance. Acknowledging the existence of inner and outer beauty is like an echo out to the universe that will come back to us, fulfilling our deepest wishes. Beauty can be found amongst chaos when we choose to find it.

If you are currently feeling the natural desire to experience romance with another, Goddess Guinevere asks you to be mindful of the beauty within and around you. Whether you are involved in a relationship that you feel may be waning or desire a new relationship, the solution is to focus on beauty. The energy of romance is approaching you and, if you are receptive, you will feel it. Allow the gift of romance to filter through your day. Know that you are worthy of being loved by yourself and by someone special.

Stop waiting for romance, the power of romance is in the present moment.

If you have asked a specific question, the answer may be to see the beauty in the situation.

Lesson

Attracting romance by experiencing it in the moment.

Power Choice

- Bring fresh flowers into your home.
- Write a list of the qualities you would like to attract in a partner or, if already in a relationship, how you would like to see the relationship improve.
- Declutter your bedroom; the far right-hand corner when you enter the room is your Feng Shui love corner, so keep it clear and vibrant.
- Create a romance altar. Decorate the altar with pink candles and ornaments that have romantic value to you.
- Call on the romance angels and Goddess Guinevere for assistance.
- Focus on self-love.

Momentary Meditation

Imagine you are standing with Goddess Guinevere in a field of red roses. You pick a rose and breathe in its sweet perfume. As you exhale, you state your romance wish to the universe.

Affirmation

My life is full of romance and beauty.

Liz's Comments

When I received this message, the vision of Guinevere was accompanied by a strong feeling of upliftment. In that moment, I had an epiphany of what romance was. It is light, it is love, it is joy.

Our understanding of romance has been shaped by our experiences, Hollywood movies, romance novels, and the media. One can be made to feel like a loser if their romantic life does not fit into what is normal or unrealistically perfect. An example is the celebration of Valentine's Day. This can accentuate feelings of loneliness if you are single and potential disappointment if you are in a relationship and your partner does not respond how you expect them to.

I sensed this message is guiding us to look outside the square of what we should expect in romance and focus on the joy romance brings. By doing so we have something to offer our partners rather than seeking only to receive. Guinevere reminds us that romance starts from the inside and spreads outwards and encourages us to love thyself.

MESSAGE 29

———•❋•———

Grounding

Messenger

A Viking

Flying starts from the ground.
The more grounded you are, the higher you fly.
– J R Rim

Vision

A Viking thrusts his sword into the rocky ground, with vigilance.

Message

The Viking has appeared to you today to assist in grounding your energy. He is here to remind you that we live in a practical world where we need to be present and aware.

It seems your current schedule is demanding. When we multi-task, we focus on thinking, analysing and problem solving. The overload of brain power depletes our bodies and, potentially, anxiety can take over.

Common symptoms of anxiety can be insomnia, inability to focus, tightness of the chest, feeling like we can't breathe, and vertigo. It is interesting to note that in Chinese medicine, vertigo (dizziness) is described as *too much wind in the head*.

Spirit advises that you slow down. Consciously relaxing for even five minutes during the day will have a positive impact. Once your needs are met, you can return to your responsibilities, coming from a place of peace, and your affairs will run smoothly.

Whatever issues you currently face, the message is to take a grounded approach and heed practical advice. If you have asked a specific question, the answer lies in taking time out to quieten the mind and then re-ask the question. You may see things in a new light.

Lesson

Learning to find balance between the body, mind and spirit.

Power Choice

- Focus on your breathing.
- Spend time barefoot.
- Have a massage.
- Practise yoga.
- Spend time with trees and Mother Earth.
- Listen to drumming music; alternatively play a drum.

Momentary Meditation

Relaxing the body, begin to focus on your breath. Take one deep breath in through your nose right down into your abdomen and release through the mouth. Repeat twice, and finish with the affirmation below.

Affirmation

I am balanced in mind, body and spirit.

Liz's Comments

I once took myself to the emergency department of the local hospital, convinced I was having a heart attack. I remember the nurse's amused smile as she shot a sideway glance to her co-worker. I was handed a brown paper bag and instructed to breathe into it. Apparently, I was having an anxiety attack but the feeling of impending doom, another anxiety symptom, was real to me at the time.

Our society is a demanding environment. It is important we support ourselves by knowing that it is okay to attend to our needs first. This is challenging when many of us have been taught to put others first. I have even raised my own children in that way, repeating the pattern of my own childhood.

As I have aged, I have improved my self-love habits and I am forever learning. I like to make small gestures for myself to remind myself I am lovable. The other evening, I left a flower by my computer before I went to bed. When I went into my office the next morning, the flower was like a love note from myself.

Looking into your eyes in the mirror and saying something kind is good practice, even though some days it is challenging to not get distracted by the latest wrinkle that has appeared. Day by day, with practice, we can heal and love ourselves more than we realise.

Personally, I find spending time in nature and practising yoga are the most grounding activities that work for me. Explore what works for you. The theme of this message is to embrace self-care, you are worth it.

MESSAGE 30

---·❋·---

Being Present

Messenger

Merlin

The point of power is always in the present moment.
– Louise L Hay

Vision

A wizard gazing into misty terrain.

Message

Your challenge is to bring your focus and attention to the present moment.

The past and the future are thieves of the present. Let past disappointments fade away knowing that in some regard there were gifts within them. Rather than looking to the future, look at the present and appreciate all that you have in this moment. Honour yourself where you are, here and now. After all, the past and the future are but an illusion as we only have now.

Merlin wants you to know that you are an amazing, complete person who has a universe within and each breath and heart beat are a gift.

You are also being asked to be present for others. There is no greater gift you can give to another than to be fully in the moment with them and to listen, without judgement.

If you have asked a question today, know the answer is in the power of the present moment. Sometimes we are not meant to know the future. Where you are at now will determine your future as what we project, we create. Invest in the now.

Lesson

Learning to stay focused in the now.

Power Choice

- Avoid trying to control outcomes.
- Spend time with people who are special to you.
- Be aware of simple pleasures.
- Spend time in nourishing environments that support peace.
- Be grateful for what you have now.
- Meditate on your breath by focusing on each inhalation and exhalation.
- Simplify your life.

Momentary Meditation

Choose a picture or photo that you find beautiful. Take a deep breath and keep your focus on the picture, noticing its intricate beauty for at least a minute, or longer if you desire. When your mind wanders, gently bring your focus back to the picture.

Affirmation

The power is always in the present moment.

Liz's Comments

I used to think that being in the moment was focusing totally on whatever was going on around me in the external world. When I first heard this *being in the now* concept I was chopping carrots so I decided to keep repeating, *I am chopping up carrots, I am chopping up carrots.* As you can imagine, I quickly became bored and couldn't keep it up.

So what is *being in the present*, I asked myself and the universe. Over time, I have been shown that it is actually about being present on the inside which then filters out to my day- to-day life when I am in the *now* state of mind.

To me, it means not stressing too much about outcomes. It means being grateful for what I have in the present and extracting as much joy as I can from any given moment. It means gaining pleasure from the simplest things and having faith that I do have a place in our vast universe.

I have not yet mastered this, maybe someone on the planet has, but more and more I get streams of time when I do feel like this. Being in the now is definitely something to aspire towards, one moment at a time.

MESSAGE 31

Breaking Ice

Messenger

Snow Queen

The best and most beautiful things in the world cannot be seen
or even touched. They must be felt with the heart.
– Helen Keller

Vision

A wise woman covered in snow, with a crystal staff in hand, stands
on the peak of a snowy mountain.

Message

The ice around your heart is melting. Your emotions may feel like
an avalanche of feelings tumbling deep inside. Perhaps you feel
overwhelmed, or overjoyed. Whatever the case, feelings can be
intense at this time.

Any feelings you have kept to yourself for some time are now exposed and cannot continue to take up space in your heart. It is time for emotional detoxing.

The Snow Queen's message is one of reassurance that you are ready for this now in a way you would not have been twelve months ago.

Although things may feel turbulent at present, there is encouragement from Spirit to surf the waves and accept and embrace all feelings, regardless of whether you consider them good or bad. Becoming whole involves accepting our shadow side.

If you have asked a specific question today, the answer is to look within and own your true feelings before moving forward.

In the near future, the storm will pass and new clarity will dawn on a crystal clear horizon.

Be brave, accept what is.

Lesson

Acceptance of all feelings, becoming whole.

Power Choice

- Express your feelings through journaling or speaking to trusted allies.
- Express yourself creatively.
- Use music as a healing tool.
- Seek out emotional healers such as counsellors.

- Use flower essences for emotional imbalances.
- Be open to experimenting with healing techniques.

Momentary Meditation

Imagine you are sitting on a beach watching the waves.

As the waves come in, breathe in. As the waves go out, breathe out, with the intention of releasing tension and stress.

Affirmation

I am whole, I am at peace with my feelings.

Liz's Comments

When the Snow Queen entered my vision, the hairs on the back of my neck stood up. I instinctively knew she meant business. The Snow Queen's gift to you today is unique. Boundaries can now be dissolved and long standing emotional issues can be resolved.

Our belief systems can be obstacles in the course of breaking through our limitations. The Snow Queen enters your life today to offer you a wild card. The power is bestowed upon you to cut easily through issues that may have previously seemed daunting.

When a relationship of twelve months ended suddenly, I was totally devastated. I cried for a week. Walking down the street feeling dazed and confused, I wandered into a health food store and was drawn to the flower essences on sale. I noticed there was an essence specifically for mending a broken heart. I purchased the essence and took it as directed.

Two days later I woke up and felt totally refreshed, re-energised, and absolutely accepting of the relationship ending. Part of me was cynical and thought it was too good to be true. However, I could not deny how I felt and embraced the relief of feeling like myself again.

Healing can happen quickly if we allow it. There are no standard rules for how healing should take place and every person and situation is unique. The message today is that the Snow Queen can assist you in moving forward with courage and grace. Your challenge is to accept her gift and be open to healing outside your previous experiences.

MESSAGE 32

Spiritual Shifts

Messenger

Serpent

Trust in your Inner Power and miracles will happen.
– Deshwal Sachin

Vision

A large, thick Serpent, with lime and black stripes, crawls along the seabed.

Message

The Serpent brings the message that deep-healing spiritual shifts are now occurring in a way that may be new to your conscious self. The hard work you have been doing on inner levels is now showing much like seeds sprouting through rocky soil. You have built strong and sturdy foundations and there is a new source of spiritual power that you can now tap into.

Externally in your life, some unexpected events may now arise, some of which are out of your control. Draw on your inner wisdom to handle these events, rather than following impulsive or old ways of dealing with things. This is a new era in your life where you will approach life from a deeper stance with increased mindfulness and awareness.

The Serpent advises to remain observant at this time and keep a detached perspective. Allow the marriage of clarity and feeling to embrace you, making the way forward clear.

Celebrate your growth. You have arrived at an auspicious yet rewarding time in your life.

Lesson

Tapping into spiritual power.

Power Choice

- Take time for reflection.
- Spend time near water or indulge in water-based therapies.
- Call on the energy of the Serpent for strength and clarity.
- Go deep in your meditations.
- Manifestation techniques activate with ease at this time.

Momentary Meditation

Breathing deeply, relaxing – visualise yourself on a seabed. The Serpent approaches and you peacefully unite with its energy.

The Serpent has a message for you, what is it? Accept the first thought that comes to mind, and give thanks to the Serpent.

Affirmation

It is safe to be in my spiritual power.

Liz's Comments

Spiritual awakenings are often triggered by major life events, but not always. It may be a chance encounter with an individual who has a profound effect on us, or simply something we heard in conversation that ignites a realisation.

We are all powerful. We all possess a soul which is made from indestructible matter but often it is covered in debris from experiences we could not fully process. This message is to alert you to the fact that your soul is throwing aside the debris and is ready to reveal some of its infinite power.

You may have had many incarnations to arrive at this point and it is a time to be celebrated, not feared. Accept that you can be a channel for divine energy and that it will affect your life positively, but inevitably will affect others as well. How they respond to your soul growth is their business, not yours. You are encouraged to remain true to yourself.

I have had several major spiritual awakenings in my life and hope to experience more. I can relate to this message and sense it is bringing wonderful news of forward movement in a way that will ultimately delight and uplift you. Your task is to be alert, receptive, and to acknowledge the truth in your epiphanies.

MESSAGE 33

·※·

Strength

Messenger

Sunflower

Dig deep and empower yourself today.
Stand in your inner strength. Be uniquely you.
– Amy Leigh Mercree

Vision

A Sunflower stands tall, stretching into a vast blue sky.

Message

You may be faced with some practical decisions that require self-confidence and strength. This message is a reminder that under the surface of your chattering mind lays a wisdom you can tap into to navigate your way forward. Your task is to extract the *knowing* within you and apply it to your practical world.

Although you may be temporarily confused at present, you are encouraged to follow your inner guidance and not the advice of others, regardless of their kind intentions.

Whatever your query is today, you are advised to take a practical approach. If you need to communicate with someone, then do so. If you need to research a possibility you are feeling guided to, do so. If you need employment, take action such as updating your resume.

There is a saying that *God helps those who help themselves* and sometimes, if we take one step towards helping ourselves, the universe will take a thousand.

Lesson

Learning to utilise your inner strength and weave it into your practical life.

Power Choice

- Seek practical advice from experts, if needed.
- Commit to practical plans that feel intuitively right.
- Call on nature spirits for assistance with grounding and manifestation.
- Connect with the energy of the Sunflower.

Momentary Meditation

Sitting quietly, bring your focus to the earth beneath you.

Take a breath in, drawing up the nurturing energy of Mother Earth. Breathe out. Do this several times.

Affirmation

It is safe to draw on my inner power and strength.

Liz's Comments

You are being reminded of your inborn inner strength that is now emerging to serve you at this time. By connecting with your innate self-confidence you can be victorious even in the most complex situations.

When I relocated interstate, friends and family advised me it would not be a smart move. They said I would be leaving behind a lovely home, a growing business, and a support network. Although they made valid points to consider, I chose to trust my inner guidance and make the move. I certainly did have to draw on an inner strength I didn't know I possessed. I was a single mother of a three-year-old and the move was challenging. I trusted my gut feelings, drew on my strength and made some big practical decisions. Everything worked out well in the long term.

What is happening in your life now that may require you to stand up for yourself and claim what it is you need, even if others do not agree? Spirit is encouraging you to be your own supporter and has total faith that you can move mountains if you need to.

MESSAGE 34

Threads of Hope

Messenger

Angel of Compassion

Hope is like the sun, which, as we journey towards it,
casts the shadow of our burden behind us.
– Samuel Smiles

Vision

An angel covered in sparkling pink light.

Message

Just as a waterfall has layers that can be glimpsed, so does the weaving of hope throughout our lives. We hope for an outcome of happiness, joy, and abundance but what we really want it is to feel connected, to feel complete, and whole. Ironically, we are born complete, a perfect package and all we need lies within us.

This message reassures you that external obstacles and disappointments are short-lived and serve a purpose that may or may not be obvious. Hope is a powerful feeling that leads to positive thoughts and, in turn, positive manifestations. Focusing on hope will boost your energy and enthusiasm, and strengthen your Spirit.

Exercise compassion for yourself and others. Laying blame is wasted energy. The threads of hope are part of the tapestry that embodies your soul and you have the power to turn hope into solid forms that will serve your soul.

Lesson

Learning to recover from setbacks through connecting with your deeper self.

Power Choice

- Call on the Angels of Compassion for help and guidance.
- Write a gratitude list to help achieve a positive mind set.
- Name what it is you hope for, to aid the power of manifestation.
- Acknowledge and honour past hopes that have materialised.

Momentary Meditation

Sitting quietly, visualise an angel surrounded by pink sparkling light. She holds open a white, silk bag embedded with jewels.

Affirm what you hope for and see the words going into the bag. The angel blesses you and takes them back to the angel realm for manifestation to occur.

Affirmation

All my hopes that serve me manifest beautifully in perfect timing.

Liz's Comments

When I experienced the vision of the angel accompanying this message, I felt an upliftment around my heart centre as though someone had put a human hand, made of light, into my chest which emanated joy.

Hope is the fuel that drives us to aspire to desired outcomes. Hope allows us to dream and utilise our power of vision. This is a message to remind us to honour the energy of hope and to recognise its divinity.

I hope for a peaceful passing when my time comes to make my transition to the other side. Although there are no guarantees that will happen, it certainly gives me comfort to think that it's a possibility. A life without knowing the power of hope would seem to be a bleak one.

I am sending the power of hope to all who read this message knowing that its power will bring rays of light into your life, where needed. Do not give up, hope will hold your head above the water of challenges that currently surround you.

MESSAGE 35

—•❋•—

Discernment

Messenger

Albatross

Always go with the choice that scares you,
because that is the one that will help you grow.
– Caroline Myss

Vision

A large Albatross, wings open, preparing for flight.

Message

You have outgrown a current situation in your life although part of
you may be in denial.

If you are feeling frustrated, bored, and drained in regard to a
specific situation – possibly a relationship, home situation or job –
these are signs that the situation has served you and it is now time
to open your wings and fly.

This message brings awareness to the power of your choices. It is a time where only you can make decisions to improve your life. This message is about taking risks, going outside your comfort zone, and shaking up routines, habits, thoughts, and actions.

Be positive! You can now choose to move forward to new and exciting destinations. The time is right and you will find a team of Spirit Guides and angels ready to assist you.

Do not harbour ill feelings about your current situation. Be grateful for the learning it has brought you. Count your blessings and move on.

This message may also mean you are about to travel or are being encouraged to create travel plans.

Lesson

Discernment, knowing when it is time to move on.

Power Choice

- Consciously acknowledge the positive lessons that have occurred through your outdated situation.
- Write a gratitude list.
- Plan a vacation.
- Be aware of signs from the bird kingdom.

Momentary Meditation

Either visualise or literally light a candle. Place your focus on the candle as you simultaneously take a few deep breaths.

Repeat the affirmation below either mentally or aloud.

Affirmation

I move forward with comfort and ease; I am safe.

Liz's Comments

There are stages in our lives when we cannot ignore the *knowing* within that it is time to make some complex decisions to take us to the next stage of our life. This often brings up fears and anxieties. The easier choice may be procrastination.

We can live with avoidance for so long but eventually it tends to catch up with us. It may manifest in a partner leaving us, a job redundancy, a health scare or a myriad of obvious signs that we should be making changes.

This message encourages you to use your gift of free will to make some wonderful changes, regardless of whether they are small or large changes. Utilising intention is powerful.

There is now reassurance from Spirit that if you take a leap of faith, putting your best interests at heart, all will be well.

When my first marriage ended and I was a single mother, I relocated interstate. It was a huge step and one that only I could take. I prayed consistently for signs and delayed making a definite decision. I knew it felt right but I was terrified of leaving established support systems and my lovely home. I received obvious signs that it was the right thing to do, but still I hesitated.

Arriving home after a dinner party, as soon as I set foot in the house, I had an eerie feeling. My bedroom window, which I had closed, was opened high and my bedroom was in disarray. Someone had broken in and, although I couldn't find anything missing, it unnerved me. To me, it was the final sign that it was time to leave and start afresh.

To cut a long story short, it was one of the best things I ever did. I started a new life that worked out far better than I could have ever imagined. The universe will often send us a red flag if we get off track, our job is to take notice.

MESSAGE 36

·◦·❊·◦·

Treading Gently

Messenger

White Wolf

Tread softly because you tread on my dreams.
– William Butler Yeats

Vision

A white wolf with piercing blue eyes reveals itself in the dawn light.

Message

In the correct timing, passive approaches to specific situations can be more powerful than assertive ones. Playing the game of life is an art that we can continually learn with increased grace. The message of the White Wolf is to tread gently with whatever perplexities you now encounter and you will see accelerated shifts and resolutions.

There is power in sweetness, compromise, and in unconditional love. There is no need to prove your authenticity at this time as, in its raw and natural state, it is obvious for all to see.

If you have asked a specific question today the answer is to take the gentle approach and avoid forcing issues. Letting go of an anticipated outcome is recommended. It is advisable to replace it with either a well-thought-out compromise or to wait before taking any action – whatever is in accordance with the situation at hand.

Lesson

Activating passive innate power.

Power Choice

- Call on the Spirit of the White Wolf for guidance.
- Journal to invite channelled wisdom.
- Consider potential compromises.
- Ask Spirit for help to surrender any attachment to outcomes.

Momentary Meditation

Close your eyes and visualise a White Wolf.

Imagine you are sitting behind the eyes of the wolf. Ask for the answers that you are seeking.

Affirmation

My inner wisdom rises to the surface with ease.

Liz's Comments

The feeling behind the vision of the White Wolf was one of a quiet, intuitive patience.

I feel this message speaks of the power we have been given to choose how we approach any given situation. When we react without thought, it can be hit and miss. The White Wolf reminds us that there are certain times when discerning our responses can help provide positive outcomes.

So often we feel a sense of urgency to achieve immediate results, even if they are not the optimum ones. Perhaps the way of the peaceful warrior is something to consider. Our natural intuition can scan a situation we face, when we are peaceful enough within ourselves to allow it.

Timing, patience and knowing what sits right within our hearts are skills we all have, if we are open to using them.

The process of writing a book has taught me patience. Perhaps you have experienced working on a large project that often seems daunting and you wonder how you will achieve your desired outcome. Timing, patience, and faith in oneself are all part of moving forward with grace. Whatever you face right now, do it carefully and consider the most peaceful way forward.

MESSAGE 37

Relief

Messenger

Bluebird

Perhaps all pleasure is only relief.
– William S Burroughs

Vision

A Bluebird sits on a window sill, singing a beautiful song.

Message

The sweetness of the Bluebird energy sweeping into your life brings kindness, expression, and relief.

The period of metaphorically holding your breath, or waiting in anticipation, for an outcome is now ending. The winds of change now appear to create new scenarios that offer abundant consequences.

Your consistent patience and faith reward you now and you can begin to count your blessings.

You may hear of promising opportunities and good news for yourself and/or for those you love. Contact with people at a physical distance is likely at this time. Travel or planning future travel may also be relevant in your life at present.

You have a positive message to share with others, possibly in the public arena. The power of expression accompanies the Bluebird spirit and is here to support you at this time.

If you have asked a specific question today, the answer is either *Yes*, or reassurance of breakthroughs any moment, bringing a sense of relief.

Lesson

Embracing positive breakthroughs.

Power Choice

- Be open to new solutions to new problems.
- Be alert for unexpected breakthroughs.
- Answer the phone, check emails and texts.
- Consider where travel fits into your life at present.
- Ask yourself what positive message you have to share with others?

Momentary Meditation

Imagine a Bluebird is perched on your finger singing a song as you take in its beauty. The Bluebird has a message for you.

What is the first song that pops into your head? There is a message within that song.

Affirmation

I am open to breakthroughs and golden opportunities in my life.

Liz's Comments

I experienced a joyful upliftment as this message came through. I received it on a sunny Sunday, sitting in front of my computer, awaiting inspiration and guidance to write. Part of me wished I was outside enjoying the sunshine.

As the Bluebird energy came in I distinctly heard the song *Everything is Beautiful, in its Own Way* and I immediately felt a sense of gratitude for the moment. I felt the sense of relief and what that entailed as the Bluebird energy overshadowed my being.

Life is sometimes challenging, sometimes wonderful, sometimes sad, and sometimes joyful. There is such a wide range of experiences to be had and certain times for particular experiences. However, this message heralds that it is time for something wonderful.

Be assured that all is working out for the best and in divine timing.

MESSAGE 38

·※·

Variety

Messenger

Wild Flowers

Life wants you to touch, taste and see the grandeur
of the world's unfathomable variety.
– Bryant McGill

Vision

A vibrant, green field decorated with colourful wild flowers that
sing in a soft breeze.

Message

There are millions of people in the world. There are millions of
experiences to be had. Yet so often, we tend to live our lives in a
safe bubble that somehow makes us feel secure. This message is to
encourage you to go outside your bubble and make friends with new
people, and new experiences.

It may feel uncomfortable at first, but how will you know if you don't try? There is no obligation to commit to anything, however the feeling behind this message is that you may be pleasantly surprised by what awaits you outside of your comfort zone.

You may have recently found that random thoughts and new ideas are entering your mind. This is guidance from those who love you in the Spirit World, encouraging you to expand yourself through new experiences.

Is there something creative you have always wanted to try? Is there a physical activity that interests you, or a study course that has seemed appealing in the past? Would you like to learn to meditate? Is the reason you have not become involved in these things because you believe you can't do them? If you answer *Yes* to any of these questions, this message is reassuring you it is time for you to stretch yourself and encourages you to experiment more fully with life.

If you have asked a specific question today, the answer lies in being adventurous and thinking outside the square.

Stand tall, have faith and jump! Spirit will catch you!

Lesson

Inviting variety into the human experience.

Power Choice

- Make a list of life experiences you would like to have.
- Make a list of possible practical ways you could manifest these experiences.

- Ask Spirit to guide you to new experiences.
- Be aware and open-minded to new people entering your life.

Momentary Meditation

Imagine you are doing an activity you have always longed to do, even if it seems totally unlikely that it would eventuate.

See yourself succeeding in this activity. Use all of your senses and focus on how good it makes you feel. You may also want to imagine the new people you would like to meet.

Affirmation

I am open to a world of new and positive experiences.

Liz's Comments

I loved the vision of the wildflowers as they appeared with a sense of delight and joy.

We have all heard the saying, *variety is the spice of life,* yet many of us choose not to deviate from what we already know.

I can relate to this message as many times I have declined an invitation or an offer simply for fear of the unknown. There have been times when I have said *Yes* and been pleasantly surprised.

Recently I enjoyed my first snorkelling experience while visiting Hawaii. For me, it was a major breakthrough. I said *Yes* whereas in the past I had said *No!* The beautiful fish, turtles, and coral I saw were a wonderful experience and it didn't take long to get used to the breathing equipment. I felt good about myself afterwards and look forward to my next snorkelling experience.

I feel this message is asking you to be aware of opportunities that may be outside your comfort zone. I sense there are some wonderful experiences on the horizon for you, so trust your intuition and say *Yes!*

MESSAGE 39

--•❋•--

Accepting Uniqueness

Messenger

Spirit of the Swan

To love, and be loved, this is the greatest challenge
that any of us face in our lives.
– T Scott McLeod

Vision

Two swans on a still lake form the shape of a heart with their heads.

Message

It's easy to become so immersed in our own thoughts, feelings, and behaviours that we become oblivious to the perspectives and feelings of others. Finding harmony in another's rhythm is part of your quest at this time.

In the process of maturing, we are able to recognise that we are not only all unique individuals but that, at any given time, feelings and thoughts are responding and changing depending on the scenery in our lives.

This message is to alert you that someone you care about would love you to understand how things look in their world. This information will help you in your own life experience. It may influence some important decisions that are imminent. Impulsive decisions do not serve you now. Spirit encourages deeper contemplation.

If you have asked a specific question today, the answer lies in considering someone else's point of view. Someone close to you may have advice worth contemplating. Consider how any decisions you make now will affect others.

The challenge is to rise above entrenched belief systems to achieve optimum results. The universe and Spirit have deep faith that you can do this right now. Know that Spirit is supporting you at this time.

Lesson

Acceptance of the uniqueness of others.

Power Choice

- Schedule time with a person close to you to have a deep conversation.
- Contemplate what it is like to be in someone else's shoes.
- Let those you love know it is okay and safe to open up to you.
- Let go of any former judgement of others.
- Give someone a second chance.

Momentary Meditation

Imagine you are walking along a path in a botanical garden, hand in hand with someone you love.

You arrive at a lake and are in awe of the White Swans gliding on the still water. A healing takes place as you feel overwhelming peace between you and your loved one.

Affirmation

I am in harmony with those I love.

Liz's Comments

When the vision of the Swans appeared I was bathed in a sweet energy of harmony and peace between two separate entities. I instinctively knew that, in truth, the separateness is an illusion and all life is derived from the same source. This is something that each of us naturally longs to experience and occasionally glimpse.

I believe this message is guiding you to look deeper into any relationships that are meaningful to you and to approach them from a higher perspective, allowing air and movement to flow within the connection. It is a heart-warming message signalling that this is possible now.

Being open-minded, open-hearted, and compassionate will fuel your movement forward in regard to finding harmony with those you love most.

MESSAGE 40

•◊•

You Can Change

Messenger

Gecko

Those who cannot change their minds cannot change anything.
– George Bernard Shaw

Vision

Gecko sits in warm sunshine, changing colours.

Message

Sometimes we would rather die than change. According to the Buddhist philosophy, attachment is the root of unhappiness as impermanence is a reality of living. We can be attached to ways of thinking and being, even though we often justify it by convincing ourselves that these are the *right* ways or the *healthy* ways.

Stubbornness breeds infertile grounds for new growth and the message today is to ask you to reflect on the areas of your life where you are feeling stuck, and your thinking habits and processes around them.

Look outside the square of your safe boundaries you have created. Be the artist in your life, giving yourself freedom to create your unique symphony. Somewhere in your life experience you are feeling suffocated by your own choices. With the help of Spirit, prayer, and reflection you may now have epiphanies that will change the colour of your world.

If you have asked a specific question today, the answer lies in doing or viewing things differently.

Lesson

Flexibility.

Power Choices

- Acknowledge any deep *gut* feelings you have been ignoring about making changes.
- Review belief systems and question what is serving you.
- Explore self-growth techniques such as tapping or releasing-based meditations.
- Focus on beliefs that give you inner strength and confidence.

Momentary Meditation

In a relaxed state, imagine you are looking through a kaleidoscope, admiring the changing, colourful patterns.

Visualise yourself looking happy and well, merging with the kaleidoscope patterns, and feeling the joy of shifting and changing.

Affirmation

Change is fun and full of opportunities.

Liz's Comments

My mother often remarked about my stubbornness as a child and, I must confess, she is right. My stubbornness has, at times, been my ally and, at other times, my enemy. There is a balance to be found in all things when one is seeking to achieve harmony in life. It is not impossible to change our beliefs if we use awareness and self-love as our tools.

This message is hinting that you have reached a point where your resistance may not be serving you and is a gentle reminder to ultimately be kinder to yourself by making choices that invoke joyful experiences.

Save the steadfast energy for times in your life when you will need it for grounding yourself and supporting others. Now is the time to loosen up and increase your capacity to enjoy your precious time here on the planet.

MESSAGE 41

·*·

Connecting to Spirit

Messenger

Eagle

You cannot fly like an eagle with the wings of a wren.
– William Henry Hudson

Vision

An Eagle slowly circles in a clear blue sky.

Message

Prayers are heard and answered even when we fail to recognise the most obvious replies from heaven. Wherever we place our focus becomes our reality. The universe will conspire to create events that are based on our heart's desires.

Spirit asks you to analyse where your current focus lies. They ask this of you as there are signs in your life now that are a form of Spirit guidance and they want to help you recognise the language of Spirit.

Spirit is not here to judge you or indicate that you have in any way failed. Spirit only wants to strengthen the lines of communication between your conscious and higher self so that your life can be one of wonder, growth, and fulfilment.

Scan the perimeters of your life. Ignore doubt and trust the rhythm of your intuitive self. Messages and signs arrive with a distinct *gut* feeling. Whatever your query is today, the answer is right in front of you. Ask for the eyes to see clearly.

Lesson

Seeing your life through the lens of your soul.

Power Choice

- Consciously realign your energy through healing, meditation or nature.
- Ask Spirit for clear and obvious signs, and guidance.
- Believe in your gut feelings.
- Look for signs, particularly from our avian friends. Birds are messengers of Spirit.

Momentary Meditation

Imagine you are viewing your life from high above, through the eyes of the Eagle. This technique is called *shape-shifting*. Ask yourself what insights and messages emerge?

Affirmation

I receive clear guidance at all times.

Liz's Comments

How many times have we had a distinct feeling that we should or shouldn't do something, or perhaps an inner knowing that we were being betrayed, and chose to totally ignore it? We reason with our logical minds that the feeling doesn't mean anything. Perhaps we fear we will be unable to cope with the potential consequences if we acknowledge our gut feelings.

The Spirit of the Eagle is bringing you strength to face the truth in any situation you are experiencing at present. Remember that all situations we find ourselves in, no matter how complex, are opportunities to acquire wisdom, to propel our consciousness into a higher realm, and then integrate them into our day-to-day worldly experience. This may not happen immediately but, like a good wine, experience and wisdom mature with age.

When I see an Eagle circling the sky my heart skips a beat. There is something so magical about its magnificence and you can feel the power it radiates. I interpret the sighting as a sign from Spirit to remember there is always a bigger picture to any given situation. The Eagle's far-reaching vision sees all details simultaneously and then it plans its next move. We can also choose to soar above the perimeters of our daily lives and view our complexities from an objective point of view.

The night before I was initiated into the master level of Reiki, I had a vivid dream of sitting with a wise woman watching the sky. As an Eagle came into view, the wise woman turned to me and said with conviction, *You must be like the Eagle, rise above challenges and you will see the answers.* The uncanny element of that dream was that the next day, at my initiation, one of my teachers whom I had never met, was actually the wise woman in my dream!

This is the gift the Spirit of the Eagle has brought you today – fly high, observe, and trust your deep and truest feelings.

MESSAGE 42

·•-※-•·

Past and Future Lives

Messenger

White Owl

For truly we are all angels temporarily hiding as human beings.
– Brian Weiss

Vision

A White Owl in the night sky dances with a star as shimmering lights awaken the sky.

Message

There is much more going on regarding your query or your life's current events than you are consciously aware of. There is always a bigger picture to every moment of our lives and when we are meant to understand, we do, at least partly.

When we do not understand, we are thrown into the arms of faith and trust, and deep inner knowing that somehow everything works out in the bigger scheme of things.

Consider the concept that time may not be linear. The past, the present, and the future may well be one, occurring simultaneously in a timeless, yet organised, vacuum. The intelligence of the universe is beyond our limited understanding.

Karmic relationships that are as old as the sun may present themselves in your life, perhaps causing some type of inner turmoil or confusion. This is a catalyst to spring clean old beliefs, old patterns, and wounds, ultimately bringing you closer to your own divinity.

If you have asked a specific question today the answer is woven in a deeper fabric than your current understanding. Therefore, trust is your best friend right now.

Alternatively, karmic relationships may bring windfalls of luck, adventure or romance – again, to bring you closer to your own divinity. Fate is in control right now, so sit back, observe, and enjoy the ride.

Lesson

Expanding your soul through karmic relationships.

Power Choice

- Research past/future life work.
- Take extra notice of your dreams by starting a dream journal.
- Be patient and let the bigger picture unfold.

- Read between the lines in relationship issues.
- Trust your gut feelings around relationship situations.

Momentary Meditation

Before you go to sleep, get into a meditative space and have an intention for a clear dream to answer your current concerns, including that you will remember the dream. Dreaming is a wonderful way to bypass the conscious mind. You may like to write the request and put it under your pillow. If nothing happens the first night, keep repeating the process. Placing a selenite crystal beside your bed may also enhance your experience.

Affirmation

My soul knows all the secrets of the universe, therefore I trust.

Liz's Comments

White Owls have a special significance for me as it is my main Spirit Guide's name and sometimes my Guide will use the visual of the White Owl to get my attention. When this message came through it was with a force of power that went through my whole being. I sense whatever is happening in your life right now is of special significance, but you may not understand this until a later date. Think back in your life when you had an encounter that was to shape your destiny, even if you had no idea at the time. This is the feeling of this message; it is an ominous time.

I recall meeting my first husband through a mutual friend and my first impression was that he was boringly over-confident and

I certainly felt no physical attraction towards him. How could I have known the evening we met that I would be married to him for almost ten years and have a son with him?

People, places and things can alter our destiny when we least expect it, this is such a time for you. Have faith in the bigger picture.

MESSAGE 43

—•⁂•—

Persistence

Messenger

An Ox carrying a Heavy Load

Patience, persistence and perspiration make an
unbeatable combination for success.
– Napoleon Hill

Vision

Workers building the Egyptian Pyramids.

Message

Wondrous things can happen when we persevere and break through
previously-considered impossible tasks. This message lets you know
you have more powers of perseverance than you are aware of and
you can achieve so much more than you are currently envisioning
for yourself.

The power of the Ox is with you today to ground you, to encourage you, to help you to dig deep within yourself. You are being asked to reassess your priorities and your time-management skills. Where could you find more time to work towards your dreams? Ignore the doubting thoughts that insist small amounts of time add up to nothing. Small amounts of time dedicated to manifesting your true desires are like diamonds that make up a completed necklace.

If you have asked a specific question today, the answer is that there is some work in progress or that the whole picture is not yet complete. The way forward may require patience as it seems that step-by-step is the best approach.

There are times in life for certain activities, now is a time of commitment and dedication. From challenges, inner strength, wisdom, and gratitude follow.

Lesson

Understanding and utilising your own inner strength.

Power Choice

- Review time management plans.
- Reassess goals and desires.
- Commit to tackling the seemingly harder aspects of manifesting your desires.
- Consider giving yourself small rewards at different stages of achievement.
- Methodically take the step-by-step approach.

Momentary Meditation

In your mind's eye, visualise a huge tree. Imagine it when it first sprouted. Imagine how it looked at various stages of growth until it became the huge tree it is now. See your own dreams and desires, envisaging the final outcome you desire.

Affirmation

I am strong, determined, and have wonderful powers of manifestation.

Liz's Comments

When I reflect upon this message I see visions of many people on the planet working hard to make it a better place. The power of hard work coupled with positive intentions is a formidable combination where mountains can be moved.

We are consistently challenged in this life by a multitude of situations. When we resist playing the victim and claim our power through helping ourselves, the universe swings into action to support us.

I know this is an important lesson as it was particularly relevant to me in my younger years. It was one I had to repeat many times until I understood I had to be responsible, not only for my practical life but also for my own happiness.

Whatever challenges you face at present, I am sending you positive intentions and encouragement that you can do whatever you put your mind to!

MESSAGE 44

Light Heart

Messenger

Unicorn

When you do things from your soul, you feel a river moving in you, a joy.
– Jalaluddin Rumi

Vision

A unicorn plays with laughing children.

Message

This message is to encourage you to shift your mindset regarding any current anxieties or concerns to a perspective of lightness and love.

In what way could you make your life lighter? What burdens are you carrying that you may not be aware of? Are they necessary or are you carrying another's burdens through your care and concern?

It is time to focus on joyous thoughts and activities to multiply the abundance of blessings Spirit has to offer you. Spring clean your energy so that you can enjoy life to its fullest.

Consider your home environment, your employment, and your significant relationships. Do these outer influences support or drain you? If the answer is the later, gently focus on one situation or area at a time and, through taking small steps, begin to make positive changes that serve you. Reach out for support from others and the Spirit World.

As humans, we need consistent reminders that our existence on the planet is transitory and our time is limited. Our priority to experience joy and happiness is not a selfish one. To the contrary, it is selfless, as each moment of joy we experience spreads out into the world in a ripple effect uplifting not only ourselves but others. You are powerful and you can choose happiness.

Lesson

Prioritising joy.

Power Choice

- Enrol in a self-love/healing course online or in person.
- Write a bucket list.
- Say *No* to others when you want to, without taking on feelings of guilt.
- Express love to those who mean the world to you.
- Ask for help to increase the levels of joy in your day-to-day life.

Momentary Meditation

Picture yourself in your mind's eye gently riding a Unicorn through a glorious forest pathway. The scents and visions of the forest calm your soul on a deep level. Feelings of simple joy flood your being. A healing from the Spirit of the Unicorn has just taken place. Give thanks.

Affirmation

I deserve to feel lightness and joy.

Liz's Comments

Today, I took a thirty-minute walk on a country road to pick up my car from a repair workshop. As I walked along, I observed the beauty of the trees, the grass, and the crisp air. I had a deja vu feeling of being sixteen years old again, walking in the country side. I re-experienced how it made me feel, light-hearted and full of joy.

Nature brings us into the moment, seducing us with its scents, its beauty, and its encompassing peace. I naturally want to breathe deeply when I am nature with the intention of permeating my being with the outer beauty I see. All worldly concerns seem trivial in those special moments. This message is a reminder of those innocent moments where we merge with the power of Spirit so naturally in a human experience.

MESSAGE 45

—•※•—

Crystalline Energy

Messenger

Black Bear in Quartz Crystal Cave

Crystals are living beings at the beginning of creation.
– Nikola Tesla

Vision

A crystal cave filled with quartz crystals occupied by a large black bear.

Message

An ascension of energy is rushing into your life which may feel like a double-edged sword. At times you feel uplifted while other times you may be feeling exceptionally sensitive, tired, and emotional.

The message of the Quartz Crystal and the Black Bear is to reassure you that events and responses happening to you now are all part of a healing crisis that is going to pave the way to greater freedom and joy within you, allowing your most authentic self to rise to the surface.

The healing crisis in question is related to soul healing and soul retrieval. Past issues may now arise. Healing is taking place on multi-dimensional levels that the conscious mind cannot begin to logically understand. Therefore, it is a time of trusting Spirit and your inner knowing.

Crystals naturally intensify energy so do not be disturbed by your current ability to feel things at a core level. This is a natural progression in your journey here on Earth and is actually a blessing. Be aware of any crystals you are drawn to at this time for they want to connect with you.

If you have asked a specific question today, healing the situation, yourself or any people involved is part of your answer.

Lesson

Allowing the self to ascend in vibration.

Power Choice

- Crystals are your ally now, use them for healing.
- Avoid over-analysing at this time.
- Self-nurture by indulging in simple pleasures.
- Watch for signs and significant dreams.
- Nurture and embrace your new found sensitivity.

Momentary Meditation

Holding a crystal that you are attracted to (alternatively visualise it), relax your mind, breathe, and gently gaze into the crystal. Let your focus go soft and ask the crystal anything that you need to know right now that could assist you. Take notice of the first thought, feeling or vision that comes to you.

Affirmation

As my awareness ascends, my soul is healed on profound levels.

Liz's Comments

Crystals magnify energy, it is a fact. As I saw the vision of the Black Bear in the cave, I immediately felt light-headed and sensitised and knew that a healing was taking place in that moment. It almost felt like small electric shocks realigning my energy.

We all have a beautiful diamond within us that is called a soul, made from an indestructible source. Life's consistent challenges can weaken our link to our higher selves where lies an endless stream of guidance to tap into. I sensed this is the core of this message. Your vibration is now being realigned so that you can experience magical downloads from the universe. Do not fear moving forward, you are being divinely guided at this time.

MESSAGE 46

•⚹•

Elevation

Messenger

Hummingbird

Quick as a hummingbird, she darts so eagerly, swiftly,
sweetly dipping into the flowers of my heart.
– James Oppenheim

Vision

A hummingbird playfully flits in a meadow of colourful flowers.

Message

You have been working hard on your inner self whether this has
been a conscious effort or has occurred naturally over a period of
time. Dysfunctional patterns have dissolved that may have been
accumulated from childhood or past lives. You have now arrived at
a new stage of spiritual maturity.

Certain invisible chains have softened, most likely concerning the question you may be asking today. Your answer is a *Yes* - you can move forward and create new situations that resonate more accurately with who you are. Contemplate how this information relates to a current situation.

There may be a temptation to take a step backwards to a comfort zone that once existed, but the message of the Hummingbird today is to take the wisdom of the past and apply it to the present. You will find doorways and openings that will expand the self and your life around you.

Others are observing your behaviour and actions and you are teaching through example. Wherever your challenges now lie, take the higher road and allow a new sense of peace to permeate your soul.

Lesson

Acknowledging self-growth, being aware of your spiritual development.

Power Choice

- Be confident to experiment with choices, regardless of fear of making mistakes.
- Release behaviours or repetitive ideas that have held you back in the past.
- Focus on the lightness and joy that you have made room for.
- Give thanks to yourself and Spirit for the growth that has occurred.

Momentary Meditation

Visualise a Humming bird joyfully extracting nectar from the centre or a flower. Connect to the joy. Make this the focus of your meditation. Gently come back and give thanks to the Spirit of the Hummingbird. (Alternatively watch hummingbirds in action on a video and tune into their energy.)

Liz's Comments

Our lives are lived in moments and some moments are memorable for all time. I was privileged to see a Hummingbird for the first time when I was visiting Arizona. It was a novelty for me as we do not have Hummingbirds in Australia. It was only a short visit as he played around a flower outside my hotel window. My heart soared immediately and, although I had thoughts of reaching for the camera, I was frozen in a beautiful bubble of joy and did not want to jeopardise the moment by shifting my focus.

The description above of my Hummingbird experience is actually the message Hummingbird wants to bring you today. Accept joy in moments. Avoid being distracted by a multiple of choices, tasks, and responsibilities that demand your attention. Coming from that place of joy within will activate your inner intuition creating a gentler flow on the path you walk.

MESSAGE 47

·❊·

Feathers

Messenger

A Band of Angels

Feathers appear when angels are near.
– unknown

Vision

A band of angels surrounded by sparkling white light.

Message

Your angels want you to know that any challenges you face now will work out perfectly in divine timing. You are supported by invisible forces and synchronistic signs, and events will confirm this if you use your eyes to see the magic that weaves in and out of our lives.

Angels are delighted when we remember to ask them for their assistance. They love to intervene with their divine rays of help

175

but it makes it much easier when we are open to their love and ask for their assistance. They love to fill us with their reassurance and unconditional love.

Your angels know you are needing help right now and reassure you they are hearing your prayers and you will have whatever you need sooner than you think. Feathers will appear out of the blue and it will be your angel's calling card, letting you know they are with you.

Angels are amazing healers. If you have asked a specific question today, be assured that angels have heard you and have been assigned to work with you on your requests. Answers will come when you least expect it, have faith.

Lesson

Expanding your relationship with angels.

Power Choice

- From your heart, ask your angels for help.
- Write a prayer to your angels and put it under your pillow.
- Read books about angels.
- Create an angel altar.
- Ask the angels to protect you.
- Collect feathers and place them in your home, your car or place of business

Momentary Meditation

Visualise feathers raining down on you. Each feather that touches your skin is like an electric shock of love from your angels. They are supporting you and blessing you at this moment.

Affirmation

I am always safe in the arms of angels.

Liz's Comments

Some people interpret feathers as a sign from their angels, particularly the ones that make their way into the most unusual places at the uncanniest of times. To some indigenous tribes, feathers symbolise forward movement. Perhaps you have your own interpretation of feathers appearing on your path.

Spirit is aware of the personal significance feathers have to you and will use them as a way of communication that you will understand.

Parrot feathers are particularly personal to me as I feel parrots are one of my animal totems. When I find them, I treasure them as I know it is a message of reassurance. In synchronistic moments, small white feathers are my angel's calling card.

This message is to remind you of the opportunity you have to connect with angels. Angels are full of joy and are wonderful problem solvers. Know that you are supported by invisible forces that will not let you down.

MESSAGE 48

Change of Plans

Messenger

Angels of Comfort

Sometimes we let life guide us, and other times we take life by the horns.
But one thing is for sure: no matter how organized we are,
or how well we plan, we can always expect the unexpected.
– Brandon Jenner

Vision

Angels holding hands in a circle, radiating soft pink light.

Message

When things don't go to plan it may be because the universe has something better in mind. The message today is to remain optimistic as there are alternative outcomes to current situations that perhaps you have not yet envisioned. Remain open to the myriad of possibilities.

Flexibility is the key to enabling you to recognise options and clear signs from above. Spirit understands you may be disappointed that a particular outcome has not eventuated. The Angels ask you to focus on what you have learned about yourself and life through this disappointment and how it can help you, and possibly others, in the future.

If you have asked a specific question today it may be telling you that the answer is to remain open-minded as things may not be what they seem. There is sense of shifting sands and twists in the road at present so remain calm and flexible in the immediate future for the best result.

The Angels of Comfort reassure you that everything will work out for the highest good of all concerned.

Lesson

Being open and accepting of change.

Power Choice

- Reflect on recent events from an objective perspective.
- Consider how recent events have affected people around you.
- Ask yourself how have you dealt with similar situations in the past
- Be gentle with yourself while you process any unexpected challenges.

Momentary Mediation

Visualise the Angels of Comfort holding hands in a circle. They radiate pink loving light. Place yourself inside the circle. Feel and accept their healing and blessings.

Affirmation

It is safe for me to be flexible.

Liz's Comments

When I feel scared or insecure, I can be quite stubborn. I know this is a defence mechanism that gives me a sense of control. I am now wise enough to recognise that when I behave like that, it is indeed fear-based which does not serve me or anyone else. Being flexible involves trusting that Spirit has my back and that in the bigger scheme of things, everything does work out for the best.

This message speaks of disappointment which is something we all experience. Multiple disappointments can wear people down causing them to become cynical or depressed. This message reminds us that we have a choice as to how we deal with disappointment. We can view it any way we choose. From disappointment we can learn compassion for others, detachment from outcomes, and that we have more strength than we believe.

MESSAGE 49

Creativity

Messenger

Rainbow

The worst enemy to creativity is self-doubt.
– Sylvia Plath

Vision

A rainbow shines over a calm, turquoise ocean.

Message

Society's ideas of creativity are limited to a small perspective. Our souls are made of a creative fabric that can stretch wider than we imagine. We are, in fact, using our creative genius in our day-to-day lives to paint the picture of our lives through creative choice and action.

This message arrives today to remind you of your capacity to activate your innate creativity by viewing your life through a wider, colourful lens.

Consider your current external life – how could you add more colour and pizazz to it? Consider your internal self-existence – are you happy on the inside, excited about life or are you feeling drab and numb within? In what ways could you encourage more creativity into your inner perspective? These are the lines of self-inquiry that may assist you now.

The answer to any questions you are asking lies in thinking creatively and expanding your outlook. Solutions will then be forthcoming.

Lesson

Expanding your creative genius.

Power Choice

- Occupy your right brain by walking, driving, housework etc. so that the left brain is free to give you spontaneous and creative solutions.
- Consider creative writing. Set the clock for five minutes and do not allow your pen to leave the page. This method allows the subconscious to communicate on paper. Begin with one sentence and do not question what you are writing. You may be surprised at the insights you receive when you read it back.
- Brainstorm solutions to any current concerns.
- Find creative mentors to inspire you.
- Utilise colours in nature and your environment to *shape-shift* your mindset.

Momentary Meditation

In a relaxed state, imagine a brilliant Rainbow. Mentally focus on each colour for five seconds or so. Start with red, then orange, yellow, green, blue, purple, and violet. Take note of any ideas or feelings that arise while you do this.

Affirmation

I allow my creative genius to rise to the surface in myself and in my life.

Liz's Comments

I was told at school that I could not draw and I was kicked out of the school choir at eight years of age. I formed the belief that I was not a creative person. I recall a sense of disappointment in myself as I affirmed that belief and felt I was a failure in some way. I am sure many of you reading this can relate to this feeling.

Reclaiming our innate power of creativity, which I now know we all have, is a liberating and joyful experience for the soul. The universe is encouraging you to be open to this aspect of yourself. There is a part of you that knows exactly how your soul would like to express itself and you only need to allow yourself to connect with that inner passion and joy.

Do not limit your creative ideas to beliefs formed in your past, be open to the new. Allow yourself to colour outside the lines of traditional concepts of creative power. By doing this, doors will open to realities to which you were previously oblivious.

MESSAGE 50

Gatekeeper

Messenger

Archangel Michael

I call upon Archangel Michael throughout the entire day.
I request that he protect and guide me in new areas of my life.
I am supported by courage, strength and faith.
– Doreen Virtue

Vision

Archangel Michael appears surrounded by purple light, holding high his protective sword of truth and support.

Message

Archangel Michael's message is to allow him and the power of the heavens to deal with any conflict in your life. Focusing on conflict creates more conflict. Focusing on solutions, such as asking for help and taking practical peaceful action, is more fruitful and beneficial to all involved.

Archangel Michael asks you to unburden yourself and return to your natural inner-child state of being. When a child feels overwhelmed with challenges their natural action is to seek support from an adult they feel they can trust. This is a similar situation. Give your challenges to a higher power and trust that your best interests are being valued and considered.

Draw on experiences from your past and remember the lessons you learned. Whatever you face now, can you recall similar circumstances? How did you cope then? What could you have done better? You got through it and life went on. Archangel Michael brings the message of support but also instils confidence in your own capability to find positive and practical resolutions. Work in tandem with Michael as the gatekeeper of your inner happiness.

If a particular query is important now, know the answer lies in a peaceful approach and by asking the angels and the universe for assistance. Once asked, prepare and expect to learn answers.

Lesson

Learning to rise above conflict.

Power Choices

- Commune with Archangel Michael through speech, thought or writing.
- Brainstorm peaceful solutions to complex problems.
- Have faith in wisdom that emerges from deep within.
- Know that this period in your life is instilling pearls of wisdom in your soul.
- Make an effort to face issues rather than avoid them.

Momentary Meditation

In a relaxed state, visualise Archangel Michael in front of you surrounded by a soothing, purple light. He holds out his hands to you. As you touch them, all your burdens are transferred to his hands. He smiles and you know deep within that all is, and will be, well.

Affirmation

I am never alone; divine guidance comes easily to me.

Liz's Comments

There have been many times in my life I when have felt overwhelmed and unsure of what pathway to take. I feel incredibly blessed to have been aware of the help on offer from the Spirit world.

I know that our requests for help must come from a deep and honest place for the connection to higher energy to be activated.

At one intensely low point in my life, I recall getting on my hands and knees and asking for divine guidance immediately as I felt utterly lost. I had nowhere to live and no money. I was feeling confused, alone, and unsure where I fitted in. Within a few hours of asking for divine help, I received a series of phone calls that provided me with a job and somewhere to live. I was extremely grateful to Spirit and it strengthened my relationship to divine power. These new beginnings gave me a practical base to continue my spiritual development within the lessons of life.

The essence of this message is to reach out for the support that is your divine right and always know you never walk alone.

Printed in the United States
By Bookmasters